Home-Centered Gospel Learning & Living

SEEKING GREATER PERSONAL REVELATION

Loren D. Marks and David C. Dollahite

Published by the Religious Studies Center, Brigham Young University, Provo, Utah, in cooperation with Deseret Book Company, Salt Lake City.
Visit us at rsc.byu.edu.

© 2022 by Brigham Young University. All rights reserved.
Printed in the United States of America by Sheridan Books, Inc.

DESERET BOOK is a registered trademark of Deseret Book Company.
Visit us at DeseretBook.com.

Any uses of this material beyond those allowed by the exemptions in US copyright law, such as section 107, "Fair Use," and section 108, "Library Copying," require the written permission of the publisher, Religious Studies Center, 185 HGB, Brigham Young University, Provo, UT 84602. The views expressed herein are the responsibility of the authors and do not necessarily represent the position of Brigham Young University or the Religious Studies Center.

Cover design by Emily V. Rogers and Alex Socarras. Interior layout by Alex Socarras.
Cover images: Top left, top right, and bottom right photos courtesy of Intellectual Reserve, Inc. Bottom left photo courtesy of Nathan Dumlao, Unsplash.
Spine image: Courtesy of Nathan Dumlao, Unsplash.

ISBN: 978-1-9503-0432-5

Library of Congress Cataloging-in-Publication Data

Names: Marks, Loren Dean, author. | Dollahite, David C. (David Curtis), author.
Title: Home-centered gospel learning and living : seeking greater personal revelation / Loren D. Marks, David C. Dollahite.
Description: Provo, Utah : Religious Studies Center, Brigham Young University ; Salt Lake City, Utah : Deseret Book Company, [2022] | Includes index. | Summary: "In discussing home-centered worship, this volume explores both individual and family worship and draws from reports from a diverse sample of more than five hundred Latter-day Saints who have shared the challenges and barriers they have faced--and successes they have experienced. Individuals and families can establish and maintain a home-centered religious life and strengthen their conversion to the gospel by using these real-life experiences, quotes, and key findings in the social sciences"-- Provided by publisher.
Identifiers: LCCN 2022004589 | ISBN 9781950304325 (hardback)
Subjects: LCSH: Families--Religious life. | Worship. | Mormon Church--Doctrines. | Church of Jesus Christ of Latter-day Saints--Doctrines.
Classification: LCC BV200 .M37 2022 | DDC 249--dc23/eng/20220204
LC record available at https://lccn.loc.gov/2022004589

For our children and grandchildren.

Contents

ACKNOWLEDGMENTS VII

PREFACE IX

INTRODUCTION XIII
Why Did We Write This Book?

CHAPTER ONE 1
Home-Centered Pathways to Personal and Interpersonal Revelatory Experiences

CHAPTER TWO 25
Personal and Shared Revelatory Experiences

CHAPTER THREE 47
Connecting with Heaven through Individual Study and Worship

CHAPTER FOUR 69
Strengthening Faith and Conversion through Family Gospel Study

CHAPTER FIVE 85
Ideas and Encouragement regarding Family Study

CHAPTER SIX 99
Joyful, Home-Centered Family Sabbath Observance

CHAPTER SEVEN 117
Fulfillment of Prophetic Promises

CONTENTS

CHAPTER EIGHT 135
More Than Promised: Unexpected Additional Blessings

CHAPTER NINE 147
Envisioning Home-Centered Religious Life after a Global Pandemic

CHAPTER TEN 165
Enjoying Revelatory Experiences in Family Relationships

CHAPTER ELEVEN 179
Revelation and Home-Centered Ways of Gathering Covenant Israel

INDEX 191

ABOUT THE AUTHORS 197

Acknowledgments

Each of us is profoundly grateful for our wife (Loren for Sandra and Dave for Mary) and children and their ongoing support of our efforts to discover and share ideas that can bless individuals, couples, and families.

We are deeply grateful to the more than five hundred Latter-day Saints who, amid their very busy lives, have shared their experiences and ideas with us in in-depth interviews and surveys. We appreciate their humility and honesty as they have opened up their lives to us so that we might learn from them. We also appreciate the more than four hundred parents and youth from various faiths who participated in our American Families of Faith Project for sharing their thoughts and experiences about how their religion influences their marriage and family life.

In a time of great societal changes and challenges, we are grateful for the prophet and apostles of The Church of Jesus Christ of Latter-day Saints, who live in such a way that they can obtain divine revelation to guide and bless all the families of the earth. With grace and patience they and their wives make monumental sacrifices of time so that they might help other families receive the peace and comfort that only ongoing divine guidance can bring.

We are grateful to several institutions at Brigham Young University for generous funding of our research over the decades, including the School of Family Life, Religious Studies Center, Family Studies Center, Eliza R. Snow Fellowship, Wheatley Institution, and College of Family, Home, and Social Sciences. We'd also like to thank Louisiana State University for research funding.

Additionally, we are grateful to the wonderful faculty, staff, and student interns at the BYU Religious Studies Center who helped this book through the publication process, including (alphabetically) Scott Esplin, Abby Knudsen, Abby Larkins, Jared Ludlow, Julie Newman, Brent Nordgren, Joany Pinegar, Emily Rogers, Alex Socarras, and two anonymous reviewers who provided insightful and helpful feedback on an earlier draft.

We appreciate valuable feedback on an early draft from Heather Howell Kelley and Justin Hendricks, as well as editorial assistance from Maddie Wilde.

Author royalties from this book will be used to support students who participate in the American Families of Faith Project.

Preface

The purpose of this book is to help promote positive individual and family response to President Russell M. Nelson's repeated charges to members of The Church of Jesus Christ of Latter-day Saints[1] to (a) deeply engage in home-centered study, learning, teaching, and worship and (b) seek a greater degree of personal revelation. Integrating responses to these two prophetic calls encourages the Saints to enjoy and share personal and revelatory experiences with loved ones in a home and family setting. This book explores how to integrate these two important and challenging processes in synergistic ways. Religious practices such as personal and family scripture study and personal, couple, and family prayer are personal and relational means to eternal ends such as two-way communion with God and all the eternal spiritual and relational blessings that can come from such revelatory experiences.

We note that leaders of the Church refer to the new initiative they announced in 2018 as a "home-centered, Church-supported" approach.[2]

Both phrases carry great power and meaning for us. If it were only home-centered—but not Church-supported—then we would all be left to our own devices and resources. Most of us would likely find that we are not able to establish or maintain healthy, consistent patterns of home gospel living without guidance, encouragement, and support of the Church and our fellow Church members. If it were a Church-centered approach, many of us likely would not obtain the many blessings available to individuals, couples, and families who make concerted efforts to establish and maintain home-centered gospel living and learning. Home-centered, Church-supported gospel living incorporates the wide array of benefits the institutional Church provides globally, such as inspired leadership and guidance from living prophets and committed ward and stake leaders, teachers, and fellow Saints—as well as supportive materials such as *Come, Follow Me*, videos produced by the Church, instructional meetings, and other resources.

To assist us in discussing home-centered worship, we deeply explore both individual and family worship and draw from reports from a diverse sample of more than five hundred Latter-day Saints who have shared with us the challenges and barriers they have faced—and successes they have experienced. These reports include members from stakes inside and outside of Utah. They include people who are single, married, remarried, or divorced—and people with children of varying ages. These individuals also relate encouraging successes, ideas, and counsel. Finally, we present detailed discussion regarding how several specific prophetic promises are being fulfilled in their personal and family lives. Throughout the book, we also share key findings from the social sciences that shed additional light on the practice of uniting in sacred practices in our homes.

We did much of our work on this book in the days following the April 2020 general conference celebrating the two hundredth anniversary of the First Vision (perhaps destined to be known as the "First COVID Conference"). Considering the major shutdowns enacted because of the pandemic, how visionary and prophetic the three general conferences urging us toward a "home-centered Church" now seem! Our hope is that this book on home-centered worship and personal revelation will help and inspire individuals, couples, and families to build on their strengths and take additional steps along the covenant path toward deeper and lasting conversion. We also hope that the tremendous revelatory and relational opportunities provided by home-centered worship will be more apparent and that we will seek and seize chances to draw closer to those we love.

NOTES

1. In keeping with prophetic counsel, when we refer to The Church of Jesus Christ of Latter-day Saints, we will use the full name or "the Church of Jesus Christ" or "the Church." When we refer to members of the Church of Jesus Christ, we will use the following terms interchangeably: Latter-day Saints, Saints, Church members, and members.
2. See Quentin L. Cook, "Deep and Lasting Conversion to Heavenly Father and the Lord Jesus Christ," *Ensign*, November 2018, 9, 10.

INTRODUCTION

Why Did We Write This Book?

Why have we written *Home-Centered Gospel Learning and Living: Seeking Greater Personal Revelation*? On October 6, 2018, President Russell M. Nelson delivered a message of historic change at the beginning of general conference when he said,

> As Latter-day Saints, we have become accustomed to thinking of "church" as something that happens in our meetinghouses, supported by what happens at home. We need an adjustment to this pattern. It is time for a home-centered Church, supported by what takes place inside our branch, ward, and stake buildings.[1]

As we heard the Lord's servant usher in this newest revelation of change, we were encouraged and hopeful for several reasons. We have spent twenty-five years working together in exploring religion and family life through in-depth interviews with hundreds of highly religious families from many faiths. We have witnessed the many ways that healthy, home-centered religious life benefits individuals, families, and societies. Accordingly, we were excited for the ways this new home-centered initiative would magnify these blessings.

In this book, we provide edifying and inspiring examples from families of various faiths (including hundreds of families from The Church of Jesus Christ of Latter-day Saints). However, we also share quotes from other religious scholars and leaders that reflect the counsel provided by living prophets and apostles. One nondenominational Christian father we interviewed at length said:

> When as a family your hearts are pointed together toward the same thing, and it's God, then parenting and economics and space and food and disagreements and hassles and joys and celebrations and all that other stuff . . . works different, it seems different, it feels different. . . . Our family are all oriented in the same way. Christ is King, He's center, He's what it's all about. . . . Our faith informs our relationships and everything about us.

In this volume we demonstrate how home-centered individual and family gospel study, discussion, and worship can "unleash the power of families," bring "deep and lasting conversion," and yield "joyful gospel living"—to borrow the focal phrases used by Church leaders in conference addresses about this subject.[2] We hope this book helps our fellow Saints, including young adults who are single or married, those who are parenting the rising generation, and those who are grandparents, to joyfully and effectively follow the inspired counsel from living prophets to move toward a home-centered approach to gospel learning and living. We suggest that a thoughtful, faithful, and joyful approach to home-centered religious life will facilitate more Latter-day Saints having meaningful revelatory experiences that will bring lasting conversion to the gospel of Jesus Christ.

WHO ARE WE?

We are two ordinary guys who are professors in the School of Family Life at Brigham Young University (BYU). We each are blessed to be the husband of a wonderful woman and the father of terrific kids. Like most husbands and fathers, we have experienced the joys and challenges of marriage and family life. Like most believing Latter-day Saints, we have tried to live the gospel and teach gospel principles to our children, including engaging in practices such as daily couple and family prayer and scripture study and weekly home evening. And like most Latter-day Saint families, we have had our successes and failures with those practices as our families have grown up and adapted to various challenges. In other words, we are like most other active Latter-day Saint husbands and fathers—doing our best to work with our partners in striving to raise our children in love and righteousness but experiencing enough challenges to keep us awake.

In addition, we have been privileged to share an extraordinary experience together that relates closely to the recent invitations from our Church leaders. Several years ago, we discovered that in a roughly two-decade window of time, there had been nearly ten thousand social science studies published on divorce. We noted that during the same time frame, there had been only about three hundred published studies (only 3 percent as many) specifically addressing strong families and the characteristics that fostered their relational health. Since that time, it has been our aim to discover the secrets of "exemplary" families of faith.

SOME TOOLS WE WILL USE

This book was inspired by several challenges from President Russell M. Nelson—challenges that have included seeking to "come, follow" the Savior, to "hear Him," to become "exemplary Latter-day Saints," and to "diligently work to remodel [our] home into a center of gospel learning."[3] We use these challenges from President Nelson and other Apostles as the foundation of our message. As social scientists, we also seek to bring to the table the best of three additional data sets that we have spent months and years and even decades compiling—data sets that offer perspective on the vital concern of home-centered worship and family strengths. In summary, these helpful tools we will use include the following:

1. **The *Come, Follow Me* report.** This report that forms the "backbone" of this book includes surveys and comments from more than five hundred members of The Church of Jesus Christ of Latter-day Saints reporting

challenges, successes, counsel, and insights regarding their efforts to respond to the *Come, Follow Me* invitation—including reports of blessings received.

2. **The American Families of Faith national research project.** This data set is based on in-depth interviews with nearly three hundred religiously, racially, and regionally diverse families (about seven hundred persons) discussing how religion influences their marriages, parenting, and families.[4] These families offer substantial insights into practices, processes, and products of home-centered family worship that are worthy of consideration by us as Latter-day Saints.

3. **The COVID-19 and religious families study.** In chapter 9, we also share some interesting findings from a survey of 1,510 Americans (including 250 Latter-day Saints) conducted in the summer of 2020 about how individuals and families responded to the COVID pandemic in the areas of spirituality, religion, family communication, and family meals.

MAP OF THE BOOK

The first two chapters provide scriptural and doctrinal foundations for the rest of the book and share the major ideas we discuss throughout the remainder of the book. Chapter 1 presents scriptural and prophetic teachings about personal revelation, personal and interpersonal revelatory experiences, sharing revelatory experiences in a home and family setting, and prophetic teachings on the new home-centered approach to religious life in the restored gospel. In chapter 2 we focus on personal and shared spiritual experiences and how they can be facilitated by home-centered gospel living. In chapter 3 we discuss two prophetic teachings related to individual study and worship and provide ideas on how to connect with heaven through individual study and worship. Chapter 4 discusses how to strengthen faith and conversion through family gospel study. Chapter 5 provides ideas and encouragement regarding family study. Chapter 6 discusses ideas on joyful, home-centered family Sabbath observance with a focus on learning from our Jewish friends. Chapter 7 focuses on the ways that five hundred Latter-day Saints have felt President Nelson's prophetic promises regarding home-centered gospel learning being fulfilled in their lives. In chapter 8, those same Saints share additional, unexpected blessings that have come from home-centered gospel learning. Chapter 9 provides some findings from research we did in 2020 about how 1,510 individuals (from couples and families) adjusted toward more home-centered religious life because of the shutdowns resulting from the COVID-19 pandemic. Chapter 10 provides some final thoughts on sharing revelatory experiences in a home and family setting and discusses several important ways to do this that are positive and healthy. Chapter 11 focuses on two more themes that President Nelson has emphasized—participating in the gathering of Israel and following the covenant path—and how revelatory experiences can assist in these sacred activities.

CREATING OPPORTUNITIES FOR REVELATORY EXPERIENCES (CORE)

In encouraging Latter-day Saints to think differently about their family gatherings, Elder David A. Bednar said, "If members of families, as they come together, would think in terms of 'I'm preparing to participate in a revelatory experience with my family[,]' . . . I think we would *prepare and act much differently*."[5] In this book, we explore various ways to approach home-centered family gatherings in ways that can create opportunities for personal and interpersonal revelatory experiences.

At the end of each chapter, we will provide some questions to encourage personal contemplation and couple and family conversation about these issues. We also will pose three questions to encourage what we call "Creating Opportunities for Revelatory Experiences" (CORE)—opportunities that involve intentions, relationships, and activities that might facilitate revelatory experiences. We hope these questions will be helpful for individual consideration and for discussion in group settings such as couple and family gatherings and book groups.

NOTES

1. Russell M. Nelson, "Opening Remarks," *Ensign*, November 2018, 7.
2. See Russell M. Nelson, "Becoming Exemplary Latter-day Saints," *Ensign*, November 2018, 113; and Quentin L. Cook, "Deep and Lasting Conversion to Heavenly Father and the Lord Jesus Christ," *Ensign*, November 2018, 8–11.
3. See Russell M. Nelson, "Come, Follow Me," *Ensign*, May 2019, 89–91; Nelson, "Hear Him," *Ensign*, May 2020, 88–92; and Nelson, "Becoming Exemplary Latter-day Saints," 113–14.
4. We began conducting these interviews soon after September 11, 2001 (9/11), and continued the interviews until 2021. We contacted religious leaders in Christian, Jewish, and Muslim congregations across the country and asked them to recommend families from

their congregation that they considered to be excellent examples of devoted members of their faith community. We then contacted those families to ask if they would be willing to tell us about ways that their religious beliefs, spiritual practices, and faith communities have influenced their marriage and family lives. All families were dual-parent homes. More than half were from various ethnic minority communities. Families were drawn from seventeen states in all eight socioreligious regions of the nation identified by scholars. These included families from the following regions (and states): the mid-Atlantic (Delaware, Maryland, Pennsylvania), the Midwest (Ohio, Wisconsin), the Mountain West (Idaho, Utah), New England (Massachusetts, Connecticut), the Northwest (Oregon, Washington), the Pacific (California), the South/Gulf Coast (Florida, Georgia, Louisiana), and the "Southern Crossroads" region (Kansas, Oklahoma).

5. David A. Bednar, *The Spirit of Revelation* (Salt Lake City: Deseret Book, 2021), 58; emphasis added.

CHAPTER ONE

Home-Centered Pathways to Personal and Interpersonal Revelatory Experiences

As part of what President Russell M. Nelson has called the "process of restoration"[1] and what has been called an "ongoing restoration,"[2] important divine revelations have been given to the living prophets, seers, and revelators who lead The Church of Jesus Christ of Latter-day Saints. Two central themes of the prophetic ministry of President Nelson have been (1) a home-centered, Church-supported approach to religious life and (2) the importance of each Latter-day Saint increasingly obtaining personal revelation. We will discuss personal revelation, as well as what we will refer to as "interpersonal" revelation.

PERSONAL REVELATORY EXPERIENCES

In his first general conference address as President of the Church of Jesus Christ, President Nelson stated,

I urge you to stretch beyond your current spiritual ability to receive personal revelation, for the Lord has promised that "if thou shalt [seek], thou shalt receive revelation upon revelation, knowledge upon knowledge, that thou mayest know the mysteries and peaceable things—that which bringeth joy, that which bringeth life eternal" [Doctrine and Covenants 42:61]. . . .

To be sure, there may be times when you feel as though the heavens are closed. But I promise that as you continue to be obedient, expressing gratitude for every blessing the Lord gives you, and as you patiently honor the Lord's timetable, you will be given the knowledge and understanding you seek. Every blessing the Lord has for you—even miracles—will follow. That is what personal revelation will do for you.

. . . We live in a world that is complex and increasingly contentious. The constant availability of social media and a 24-hour news cycle bombard us with relentless messages. If we are to have any hope of sifting through the myriad of voices and the philosophies of men that attack truth, we must learn to receive revelation.[3]

Elder David A. Bednar of the Quorum of the Twelve Apostles has taught that we need "revelatory experiences"[4] and that the spirit of revelation "should be operative in the life of every man, woman, and child who reaches the age of accountability and enters into sacred covenants."[5] Further, a 2021 *Church News* article about the benefits of family, ward, and stake councils mentions that "spiritual preparation helps foster a revelatory experience."[6]

We will follow Elder Bednar and use the evocative phrase "revelatory experiences" to refer to spiritual communications from the Lord. Such revelatory experiences are diverse and suited to the needs of the person, marriage, or family receiving them. In other words, revelatory experiences may be cognitive, emotional, intellectual, auditory, visual, or kinesthetic. *True to the Faith* says the following about revelation:

> Revelation is communication from God to His children. This guidance comes through various channels according to the needs and circumstances of individuals, families, and the Church as a whole. . . .

> Prophets are not the only people who can receive revelation. According to your faithfulness, you can receive revelation to help you with your specific needs, responsibilities, and questions and to help strengthen your testimony....
>
> ... The witness of the Holy Ghost makes an impression on the soul that is more significant than anything you can see or hear. Through such revelations, you will receive lasting strength to stay true to the gospel and help others do the same.[7]

Revelations can be received when someone is alone in his or her "closet" (another translation of Matthew 6:6 says "inner room") or when someone is in the presence of others. When a group of people together experience the presence of the Holy Spirit, we will refer to that as a shared revelatory experience. Home-centered worship is ideally suited to facilitate the personal and shared revelatory experiences that contribute to deep and lasting conversion and help family members draw close both to God and to each other.

Revelatory experiences allow mortals to know for themselves that (a) God lives, (b) God knows us personally, (c) God loves us, and (d) God can communicate with us, including giving us personalized directions to repent, to improve, and to more closely follow His Son. Such revelatory experiences can be an anchor to our souls throughout our mortal lives. God wants to reveal insights and information to us. Indeed, according to Elder Bednar, God is continually sending revelation to us. Personal revelatory experiences allow us to come to know God and Jesus better and to learn how God thinks and feels about us personally. Such insights help us discover (or rediscover) our eternal nature and partake of the eternal life that comes from knowing the Father and the Son (see John 17:3). Even so, a fixation on only the personal can make us vulnerable to what Elder Neal A. Maxwell called the pronoun problem, too much "I, me, and mine" and too little "we and us." While personal revelation is essential for salvation, eternal life is far more than "personal"—it is familial and deeply relational.

INTERPERSONAL REVELATORY EXPERIENCES

We will now discuss four expressions of what might be called "interpersonal" revelatory experiences. We will revisit these expressions later in the book but share them here as templates. One expression of interpersonal revelatory experiences occurs when loved ones experience the spirit of revelation together. Such experiences can include sacred blessings, ordinances, shared service to others, or other profound moments that are a manifestation of the Savior's promise that "where two or three are gathered together in my name, there am I in the midst of them" (Matthew 18:20). Along with Elder Bednar, we believe that more of our family gatherings, if approached with revelatory experiences in mind, can help family members have more regular revelatory experiences that will bless them with testimony, peace, inspiration, comfort, energy, perspective, confidence, and deep and lasting conversion.

If the literally and unitedly shared revelatory experience is one form of interpersonal revelation, a second form of interpersonal revelation may occur when (under the carefully guided influence of the Spirit) one person shares true things that have been revealed to him or her through the Spirit with a carefully selected other person—things that the prophet Nephi called "the things of my soul" (2 Nephi 4:15). On one hand, the Savior repeatedly admonishes us to use care, wisdom, and inspiration in relating sacred experiences to others who are not prepared to accept or appropriately honor them (see Matthew 7:6; 3 Nephi 14:6). Indeed, there are revelatory experiences that we (or our wives) have felt impressed *not* to include in this book because of their sacred nature. On the other hand, we have all been instructed in word and by righteous example "to labor diligently to write" (2 Nephi 25:23), to record the Lord's kind dealings and tender mercies with us in order to help us enlarge our memories (see Alma 37:8) and help "our children . . . know to what source they may look for a remission of their sins" (2 Nephi 25:26). Family is a divinely appointed context for the sharing of interpersonal revelation, through experience and through both written and spoken word. The restored gospel of Jesus Christ includes marvelous doctrine about the eternal nature of marriages and families; it is also eternally important that people come to know their family members in deep and meaningful ways. Appropriate and inspired sharing of revealed testimony and experience can deepen relationships with each other and with the divine in almost unparalleled ways.

A third kind of interpersonal revelatory experience is sharing deep and sacred parts of ourselves with one another—our thoughts and feelings, our hopes and dreams, our anxieties and fears, our experiences and plans, our doubts and questions, and many other aspects of ourselves. We come to know one another when we reveal ourselves to one another. Therefore, we also use the phrase "interpersonal revelatory experiences" to describe times when people share their lives with others by sharing their inner world—the things of their souls. This can be called one's "personal sacred ground." These kinds of interpersonal revelatory experiences help build closeness between people that can strengthen their eternal relationships. We believe there are important connections and mutual influences between personal revelatory experiences (God revealing Himself to us) and these kinds of interpersonal revelatory experiences (us revealing ourselves to one another). That is, we believe that each kind of revelatory experience makes the other kind sweeter and more likely to occur. We also believe that sharing personal and interpersonal revelatory experiences strengthens relationships with God and with others (especially loved ones).

The final expression of interpersonal revelatory experience we will mention is inspired by Acts 10:38, which says that Jesus "went about doing good." What a marvelous phrase! In this dispensation, Jesus told the Prophet Joseph, "Fear not to do good" (Doctrine and Covenants 6:33). Joseph would later teach, "A man filled with the love of God, is not content with blessing his family alone, but ranges through the whole world, anxious to bless the whole human race."[8] The exalting principle here is that the Lord desires to work through us to bless others if we (like Jesus and Joseph) earnestly seek to bless them in His way. But how are we to know how to best lift, help, encourage, comfort, strengthen, and minister to a family member or another soul who needs it? Here interpersonal revelation takes a deepening and expanding plunge into the second great commandment that sets the stage for an adventure of a lifetime. If we are courageous enough to ask, "Lord, whom would you have me bless today—and how can I best do so?" then we open ourselves to a new realm of interpersonal revelation. This form of revelation invites us to share our talents, time, money, space, energy, and anything else our Heavenly Father has blessed us with in order to build up and bless others. In the social sciences, this is called generativity. In the gospel, it is called consecration and it is beautiful.

Our list of four expressions of interpersonal revelation is not exhaustive or comprehensive. However, we hope that our highlighting of (a) experiencing the spirit of revelation together, (b) relating sacred revelatory experiences with family in inspired ways, (c) sharing our sacred inner world with others, and (d) seeking to bless others in ways guided by revelation will be a source of motivation and inspiration to diligently seek out untapped but awaiting treasures in each of these expressions of interpersonal revelation.

SHARING REVELATORY EXPERIENCES

In this book, we suggest ways that Latter-day Saints can receive, enjoy, and then share personal revelatory experiences with others (especially with loved ones). We also explore how we can facilitate, welcome, share, and receive the personal revelatory experiences of our loved ones—and do so in ways that honor those experiences and the courage and love that it took for our loved ones to share their personal sacred ground with us.

We note that in the first three *Come, Follow Me—For Individuals and Families* manuals issued (from 2019 to 2021), the outline for each week's reading invites readers to consider what revelatory experiences they enjoyed during their reading of those scriptures. Each outline also invites them to record their impressions and provides space to do so. And in the *Come, Follow Me—For Sunday School* manual, the introductory materials state, "As part of *every class*, invite class members to *share insights and experiences* they had during the previous week as they studied the scriptures as individuals and families and applied what they learned."[9] Therefore, it is clear to us that Church leaders are encouraging members to seek, record, and share revelatory experiences on a regular basis.

When we use the phrase "sharing revelatory experiences," we mean to imply two things: First, individual family members who have personal revelatory experiences can share those experiences with other family members. When family members share "the things of their souls" (see 2 Nephi 4:15) with each other, it can bring a deep sense of connection and meaning. Second, when family members gather in the name of the Lord, then they may enjoy shared revelatory experiences. The Savior taught that "where two or three are gathered together in my name, there am I in the midst of them" (Matthew 18:20). In a time of increasing cultural skepticism about God and religion, sharing personal revelatory experiences with each other and having shared revelatory experiences may be among the most important things that family members can do to build both strong faith and strong family relationships.

In one sense, people share an interpersonal revelatory experience when they open up and share a part of themselves with someone else and that person "receives" what is shared. Additionally, when loved ones share interpersonal revelatory experiences that they have had with another family member, that also is sharing that experience (in the sense of telling or communicating). For example, a parent might share with a child a time when the parents first opened up to each other and shared important things about their lives with each other. This allows the child to learn about how his or her parents' relationship developed. Or a wife might share with her husband how their son opened up and shared his feelings of anxiety about an upcoming test in school and how that conversation went.

There are at least three kinds of sharing of sacred experiences with others, each more other-oriented than the last. The first is a kind of narcissistic approach to sharing, the second is a connection-oriented approach, and the third is other-focused. Or, in the words of our friend and colleague Wally Goddard, sharing to impress, to express, or to bless. The more we can share our sacred personal and interpersonal revelatory experiences in ways intended to bless others, the more likely the Spirit of the Lord will accompany our sharing.

Before moving to a discussion of doctrinal foundations for this book, we would like to share a real-life illustration of two of the expressions of interpersonal revelation shared above. To do so, we will borrow a sacred experience recorded by Loren's father, Larry:

> I remember the time [in the 1970s] our washing machine gave out. We had three kids in [cloth] diapers and I didn't [even] have money to have the thing fixed, and I certainly didn't have money for a new one, [but we still tithed]. My wife came home from running the errands . . . and there was a washing machine sitting on the porch with a hundred-dollar bill in the envelope taped to the lid, [and] boxes [of laundry detergent] from church. We don't know [exactly who] it came from . . . [but] we probably would have found out had we done the detective work. But my assessment of that was that there are some miracles that are so sacred

that to check to see whose fingerprints are on the lock to the windows of Heaven is sacrilege. Somebody obviously understood the principle of Charity where you don't let the right hand know what the left hand is doing, and they left that there for us, and God bless them!

First, we note that Larry took the time to record this sacred experience for the sake of his children. The story has also been told numerous times out loud. Second, absent in the above account but present in many of the verbal retellings to his children was a sacred promise that Larry made to God and to himself that at some future point, when his own financial situation was not so miserable, he would seek out the opportunity to likewise serve. We will follow "the principle of Charity where you don't let the right hand know what the left hand is doing" and not give specifics, but we will say that Larry and his wife, Renee, have indeed delivered on that promise. This shared experience and their example of seeking and following revelation regarding how to help others have motivated their children, including those who were wearing the cloth diapers forty-five years ago, to strive to seek out their own revelations regarding whom to bless and how to do so.

DOCTRINAL FOUNDATIONS OF HOME-CENTERED GOSPEL LIVING AND LEARNING

On the heels of this narrative of a father teaching his children, we will now seek to lay a doctrinal foundation for all that we will contemplate and consider together in this book, including home-centered worship, revelation, and family relationships.

A DIVINE PATTERN: PARENTS RECEIVE REVELATION AND TEACH THEIR CHILDREN

The recent reemphasis by living prophets and apostles on home- and family-centered teaching and learning is following a divine and ancient pattern.[10] That is, as part of the ongoing Restoration, part of what is being restored is the fulness of the divine and ancient pattern of parents teaching children about the plan of happiness and other sacred truths and commandments. This pattern began in the premortal Council in Heaven when God the Father gathered His children and taught them about His plan for their eternal progression centered in the Creation, the Fall, and the Atonement (see Abraham 3:22–28).

From the beginning, on earth there has been a pattern that includes three elements: (a) God's children call on Him through prayer, (b) God reveals sacred truths to them, and (c) they share with their posterity those sacred experiences and truths in person and in writing. In the beginning, the Lord revealed that parents should teach their children about God and their relationship to Him. Adam and Eve, our first parents, set a profound pattern for all their descendants by calling on God, receiving revelation from Him, and then diligently teaching their children about God and about what God has revealed to His children. This is recorded in the Book of Moses in the Pearl of Great Price:

> And Adam and Eve, his wife, called upon the name of the Lord, and they heard the voice of the Lord from the way toward the Garden of Eden, speaking unto them, and they saw him not; for they were shut out from his presence.
>
> And he gave unto them commandments, that they should worship the Lord their God, and should offer the firstlings of their flocks, for an offering unto the Lord. And Adam was obedient unto the commandments of the Lord. (Moses 5:4–5)

The Lord sent them a heavenly messenger to teach them how sacrifices pointed them to "the Only Begotten of the Father, which is full of grace and truth" (verse 7). God then sent the Holy Ghost to teach them that they could be redeemed from their Fall. Eve "heard all these things and was glad," and she spoke of "the joy of [their] redemption, and the eternal life which God giveth unto all the obedient" (verse 11).

Following our first parents' seeking and receiving revelation about sacred truths from the Lord, then their discussing that revelation among themselves, we are told that "Adam and Eve blessed the name of God, and they made all things known unto their sons and their daughters" (verse 12). This pattern continued as "Adam and Eve, his wife, ceased not to call upon God" (verse 16). Adam communed with the Lord and received essential doctrinal truths about the gospel. The Lord then said, "Wherefore teach it unto your children, that all men, everywhere, must repent, or they can in nowise inherit the kingdom of God. . . . Therefore I give unto you a commandment, to teach these things freely unto your children" (Moses 6:57–58).

So, from our heavenly parents and our first parents on earth, the pattern of receiving and teaching sacred truths and experiences to children was established. In reference to the children of our first parents, we are told, "And God revealed himself unto Seth" (verse 3) and "Then began these men to call upon the name of the Lord, and the Lord blessed them" (verse 4). A "book of remembrance" was kept of these sacred experiences and revelations, and "by them their children were taught" (verse 6). Finally, we are taught that "now this same Priesthood, which was in the beginning, shall be in the end of the world also" (verse 7), a prophecy that the divine and ancient pattern would be fully restored in the latter days—as it has and as it continues to be.

Prophets in the Book of Mormon: Another Testament of Jesus Christ also reflect this divine pattern. Nephi stated, "For we labor diligently to write, *to persuade our children*, and also our brethren, to believe in Christ" (2 Nephi 25:23; emphasis added), and "We talk of Christ, we rejoice in Christ, we preach of Christ, we prophesy of Christ, and *we write* according to our prophecies, *that our children may know* to what source they may look for a remission of their sins" (verse 26; emphasis added).

Because of apostasy, this divine pattern was again revealed during the dispensation given to Moses. After delivering them from bondage in Egypt, the Lord commanded the Israelites to teach their children the things He had revealed to them, including teaching them in their homes:

Hear, O Israel: The Lord our God is one Lord:

And thou shalt love the Lord thy God with all thine heart, and with all thy soul, and with all thy might.

And these words, which I commend thee this day, shall be in thine heart:

And thou shalt teach them diligently unto thy children, and shalt talk of them when thou sittest in thine house, and when thou walkest by the way, and when thou liest down, and when thou risest up. (Deuteronomy 6:4–7; emphasis added)

The Lord reiterated this principle at the beginning of the Restoration when He revealed to the Prophet Joseph Smith, "But I have commanded you to bring up your children in light and truth" (Doctrine and Covenants 93:40). Indeed, the Lord revealed that "parents . . . in Zion" were responsible to teach their children "the doctrine of repentance, faith in Christ the Son of the living God, and of baptism," or the sin would be "upon the heads of the parents" (Doctrine and Covenants 68:25).

THE ONGOING RESTORATION: "A HOME-CENTERED CHURCH" REEMPHASIZED

As we mentioned in the introduction, on October 6, 2018, President Russell M. Nelson delivered a message of historic change at the beginning of general conference when he said,

> As Latter-day Saints, we have become accustomed to thinking of "church" as something that happens in our meetinghouses, supported by what happens at home. We need an adjustment to this pattern. It is time for a *home-centered Church*, supported by what takes place inside our branch, ward, and stake buildings.[11]

Acknowledging the difficult and challenging time in which we live, President Nelson then stated,

> The adversary is increasing his attacks on faith and upon us and our families at an exponential rate. To survive spiritually, we need counterstrategies and proactive plans. Accordingly, we now want to put in place organizational adjustments that will further fortify our members and their families. . . .
>
> This morning we will announce a new balance and connection between gospel instruction in the home and in the Church. We are each responsible for our individual spiritual growth. And scriptures make it clear that parents have the primary responsibility to teach the doctrine to their children.[12]

President Nelson was announcing changes intended to bring the Church and its members into even greater harmony with the divine pattern discussed earlier. Along these same lines, Elder D. Todd Christofferson explained, "Beginning with Adam, the gospel of Jesus Christ was preached, and the essential ordinances of salvation, such as baptism, were administered through a family-based priesthood order." He went on to teach that

> we must remember that in the beginning, the Church was the family, and even today as separate institutions, the family and the Church serve and strengthen one another. Neither supplants the other, and certainly the Church, even at its best, cannot substitute for parents. The point of gospel teaching and priesthood ordinances administered by the Church is that families may qualify for eternal life.[13]

Home, not the ward building, is central—and foundational, and fortifying efforts are best made there. All of this seems to harmonize with the 1924 observation of sociologist James E. McCulloch that "no other success can compensate for failure in the home."[14] David O. McKay found sufficient truth in these words to share them in general conference on two occasions (1935 and 1964), and their relevance has increased, not decreased, in the century after McCulloch penned them.

PROPHETS DELIVER "THE PLANS"

Following a reminder that parents hold the fundamental and "primary responsibility to teach the doctrine" in their homes,[15] President Nelson explained in his conference message, "All members of the Council of the First Presidency and Quorum of the Twelve Apostles are united in endorsing this message." He continued, "We gratefully acknowledge the inspiration from the Lord that has influenced the development of the[se] plans." President Nelson then testified:

> My dear brothers and sisters, I know that God lives! Jesus is the Christ! This is His Church that He directs by prophecy and revelation to His humble servants. I so testify in the name of Jesus Christ, amen.[16]

What were the new "plans" informed by inspiration from the Lord? Elder Quentin L. Cook delivered the news of a shortened, two-hour Sunday church meeting schedule and explained that this adjustment was designed to facilitate additional time for "home-centered, Church-supported gospel learning." The desired "purposes and blessings" of the related changes included

- deepening conversion to Heavenly Father and the Lord Jesus Christ and strengthening faith in Them;
- strengthening individuals and families through a home-centered, Church-supported curriculum that contributes to joyful gospel living;
- honoring the Sabbath day, with a focus on the ordinance of the sacrament; and
- helping all of Heavenly Father's children on both sides of the veil through missionary work and receiving ordinances and covenants and blessings of the temple.

Elder Cook then urged that the new Spirit-directed pattern of home-centered learning "needs to influence more powerfully family religious observance and behavior and personal religious observance and behavior." Speaking on behalf of his brethren in the Quorum of the Twelve Apostles and the First Presidency, he then stated, "We know the spiritual impact and the deep and lasting conversion that can be achieved in the home setting." In a manner that set the tone for much of what we share in this book (prophetic teachings supported by social science findings), Elder Cook next addressed a valuable insight gained from social science research regarding deep and lasting conversion by explaining,

> Years ago, a study established that for young men and women the influence of the Holy Ghost most often accompanies individual scripture study and prayer in the home. Our purpose is to balance the Church and the home experiences in a way that will greatly increase faith and spirituality and deepen conversion to Heavenly Father and the Lord Jesus Christ.[17]

Please note Elder Cook's emphasis on "individual scripture study and prayer in the home."

Although Elder Cook did not offer a reference to a specific research study, The Church of Jesus Christ of Latter-day Saints has its own Correlation Research Division that has used social science methods to examine many related issues. Additional supporting social science research by BYU professors Brent Top and Bruce Chadwick exploring Latter-day Saint teens from across the United States has similarly summarized, "One of the most important insights we gained is the need for teens to pray and study their scriptures on their own." Top and Chadwick went on to explain that in their national study, they

> were quite surprised to discover that many of the teenagers felt no need to say their own personal prayers or read the scriptures by themselves, because they felt it was enough that they were doing it with their families. Teenagers who pray and read scriptures not only with their families but also on their own will have greater spiritual strength than those who do not. It is important for families to do these things, but in order for youth to truly internalize the gospel they must pray and study individually in the quiet and privacy of their own space. Family prayer and scripture study, as important as they are, are more *external* activities, whereas personal prayer and scripture study become more *internal*.[18]

Like President Nelson's and Elder Cook's remarks, this social science finding from Top and Chadwick indicates that deep and lasting conversion is most likely to be founded on both personal *and* family study and worship. But does this extra dimension of "internal," personal worship matter enough that it seems to measurably influence other areas of a teenager's life? Yes. Top and Chadwick reported:

> The youth in our study who exercised faith in the Lord by consistently and conscientiously communing with their Heavenly Father in personal prayer showed greater strength to resist many of the peer pressures and temptations of the world. Similarly, those teens who also personally studied the scriptures on a regular, if not daily, basis evidenced significantly lower levels of unworthy behavior [for example, alcohol and drug use and sexual activity].[19]

There is something synergistic that happens when individual devotion and familial devotion combine in a home—and in spiritual life. Gospel learning, divine insight, observed and lived experience, and social science research findings have combined to make the Brethren acutely aware of this reality. These evidences—in particular the scripturally based doctrinal foundation for parents teaching children the gospel—help explain the importance of "home-centered" efforts urged by living prophets and apostles.

So, what is the detailed plan to maximize the powerful combination of individual and family worship? Although Elder Cook referenced *Come, Follow Me*, the structure and outline he offered were simple and minimalist. He explained:

> In the home-centered, Church-supported portion of this adjustment, there is flexibility for each individual and family to determine prayerfully how and when it will be implemented.[20]

Rarely has a major Church change been made with such expansive flexibility—or with the promise of such "extraordinary" blessings. Elder Cook asked, "What do these adjustments mean for members of The Church of Jesus Christ of Latter-day Saints?" He suggested:

> We are confident that members will be blessed in extraordinary ways. Sunday can be a day of gospel learning and teaching at church and in the home. As individuals and families engage in family councils, family history, ministering, service, personal worship, and joyful family time, the Sabbath day will truly be a delight.[21]

The "delight" and "extraordinary" blessings referenced by Elder Cook include, first and foremost, deep and lasting conversion. Indeed, a careful study of Elder Cook's address, entitled "Deep and Lasting Conversion to Heavenly Father and the Lord Jesus Christ," reveals that he explicitly referenced the sacred aim of *conversion* no fewer than ten times.[22] Elder Cook stated:

> The goal of these adjustments is to obtain a deep and lasting conversion of adults and the rising generation. The first page of the individual and

family resource points out: "The aim of all gospel learning and teaching is to deepen our conversion and help us become more like Jesus Christ. . . . This means relying on Christ to change our hearts. . . . True conversion requires the influence of the Holy Ghost" [*Come, Follow Me —For Individuals and Families*, v].[23]

Elder Cook then underscored the importance of cooperation and healthy flexibility by saying, "We trust you to counsel together and to seek revelation for implementing these adjustments—while not looking beyond the mark or trying to regiment individuals or families." Recently published social science indicates that one feature of "exemplary" religious families of various faiths is that they seem to find a balance between firmness, structure, and consistency on one hand while maintaining flexibility, adaptability, and creativity on the other.[24] This healthy blend can yield delight instead of drudgery.

In our work, we have been blessed by seeing how often social science, doctrine, and prophetic teachings align. Even so, our motivation for emphasizing this divine and doctrinal pattern is not based on social science but on scriptural and prophetic teachings about the doctrine that God has revealed and our trust in his doctrinal pattern. Elder Christofferson taught, "The social science case for marriage and for families headed by a married man and woman is compelling. . . . But our claims for the role of marriage and family rest not on social science but on the truth that they are God's creation."[25] The divine pattern of parents teaching children is God's creation, ordained and commanded by God.

In the concluding address of the October 2018 conference, President Nelson exhorted the Saints:

> The new home-centered, Church-supported integrated curriculum has the potential to unleash the power of families, as each family follows through conscientiously and carefully [strives] to transform their home into a sanctuary of faith. I promise that as you diligently work to remodel your home into a center of gospel learning, over time *your* Sabbath days will truly be a delight. *Your* children will be excited to learn and to live the Savior's teachings, and the influence of the adversary in *your* life and in *your* home will decrease. Changes in your family will be dramatic and sustaining.[26]

In the words of one member, "We don't simply go to church, we *are* the Church!"

WE CAN LEARN FROM EXEMPLARY FAMILIES

Shifting back to our own work, we were pleasantly surprised that President Nelson chose "Becoming Exemplary Latter-day Saints" as the title and theme of his concluding October 2018 address. The exemplary families of faith we have had the pleasure of interviewing opened their homes to us and shared their stories with us. They discussed their successes, their failures, their challenges, their beliefs, and their worship. They invited us onto their sacred ground.[27] Namely, many of these exemplary persons, including wives/mothers, husbands/fathers, and eighty-four youthful daughters and sons (10–25 years old), discussed how they came to develop a connection (or even a relationship) with God through personal, couple, and family worship. What has worked, what has failed? What has been magical, what has been mundane? What has been beautiful, what has caused bitterness?

Our own research explored the question of "When is it time for parents and youth to discuss spiritual and religious matters?" We discovered the answer was *often . . . if* the conversations are youth centered (rather than parent centered). We explored the question "When is it time for parents to preach?" We discovered the answer was *rarely*. A strong parental example is far better than preaching. We also explored the question of "When is it time for parents to listen?" We discovered that the answer that many wise parents gave (and that most youth agreed with) was "far more often than most parents do."[28] Whether families were teaching us about sacred religious practices, about balancing firmness and flexibility, about agency and accountability, or about the spirit and nature of healthy parent-child dialogue about religion, our hope has been that by carefully examining exemplary religious families, all could benefit and learn from their successes and their challenges.

Therefore, when President Nelson and Elder Cook commenced October 2018 general conference with a call for powerful home-based learning as a vital pathway to joyful gospel living and deep and lasting conversion, we were profoundly interested. When President Nelson concluded the historic conference with his call to us to "unleash the power of families" and to become "exemplary Latter-day Saints," we were excited for the blessings we knew would accrue for individuals and families from heeding this inspired prophetic counsel. We have seen a rich, colorful, and diverse array of families inside and outside the Church of Jesus Christ—and we have seen that when individuals and families learn of, speak of, and commune with God in their homes, life's challenges do not stop, but that authentically lived faith makes it possible for even their afflictions to be consecrated for their gain (see 2 Nephi 2:2).

However, those who have made the intentional journey to joyful and faithful family life have repeatedly told us that the blessings of this promised land are not to be won easily or quickly. The realities of the cultural wilderness that we all inhabit, including increasing wickedness, materialism, individualism, and distractions in the form of an array of enticements, mean that it requires great personal and family efforts to cross over into that promised land. In the words of leading marital researcher and therapist William J. Doherty, the single greatest danger to marriage and family life may simply be the wear and tear of everyday living.[29] Indeed, the perennial challenges of "the world," our own selfish desires, societal distractions, and the chaotic and disintegrating influences of everyday life all require vigilance and consistent efforts to overcome. Even so, we have seen the truth of President Nelson's words—that those who "feast upon the word of the Lord and apply His teachings" are indeed blessed with "increased faith . . . and patience to endure [their] personal challenges in life."[30]

This book provides many examples of faithful individuals and families who are living imperfect but exemplary lives of religious devotion. We hope the examples provided here, from our fellow Saints as well as our friends of other faiths, will inspire you and help you learn various ways "to unleash the power of families" in your own lives and homes. We particularly hope that the examples from many individuals and families found in these pages will help the rising generation.

Patterns of meaningful religious practices are important to establish and maintain. But research, including our own, has indicated how important it is to (a) focus on the quality of relationships along with the quality of practices and rituals and to (b) balance what we call religious firmness with religious flexibility.[31] But more than just providing a possible menu of home-centered religious practices from which to choose, we strive to explore ways of engaging in study and worship (both individually and with others) that are more likely to result in joyful gospel living.

To enable persons and families to experience deep conversion and joy, we have found that it is important to help children learn the *whys* of religious observance and not just the *whats* and *whens*. This includes focusing on the things that matter most (for example, our eternal parents and divine heritage, our Savior, the plan of happiness, the Atonement, the Restoration, and our covenants). As we previously discussed in the section on the divine pattern, parents' teaching children about core doctrines and sharing their own sacred revelatory experiences with them are among the things that matter most. Further, this sharing can be profound and meaningful (see Moses chapters 5 and 6).

ALL FAMILIES ARE IMPERFECT (INCLUDING OURS)

We have spent our professional careers exploring the ways that religious beliefs, spiritual practices, and faith communities influence marriage and family life. We have spent our personal lives—at least on our good days—trying to live and teach the gospel in our own homes and families. Among the hundreds of families whom we have been privileged to interview for our research (and among hundreds of families we have been privileged to associate with in The Church of Jesus Christ of Latter-day Saints), we have observed many strong and healthy families of faith. None of these families—including our own—is perfect. All families—including our own—are made up of imperfect people doing their best to live their lives, address personal and relational challenges, come to know God and each other, and resist personal sin and weaknesses. Every marriage and family—including our own—involves some degree of disappointment, grief, and longing for things to be better. This too is by divine design, since imperfect families make up the "earthly homes" that help us learn to overcome opposition and challenges.[32]

Part of what it means to be part of an imperfect family (and an imperfect community of Saints) is the potential for human expectations to take precedence over divine doctrines. Elder Dieter F. Uchtdorf taught that following the Savior's commandments is the essence of being a disciple of Christ, but then he cautioned,

But this may present a problem for some because there are so many "shoulds" and "should nots" that merely keeping track of them can be a challenge. Sometimes, well-meaning amplifications of divine principles —many coming from uninspired sources—complicate matters further, diluting the purity of divine truth with man-made addenda. One person's good idea—something that may work for him or her—takes root and becomes an expectation. And gradually, eternal principles can get lost within the labyrinth of "good ideas."[33]

With all of this said, as social scientists, we believe that there are both warnings and wisdom that can be gathered and garnered from careful observation of human failures and successes. As disciples of Christ who are imperfectly striving to be "all in," it is our further and deeper conviction that earnest study of the scriptures and sincere effort to sustain and follow the living prophets can help imperfect families—including yours and ours—become far more than they could without inspired guidance. In this book, we imperfectly but sincerely strive to convey prophetic, scriptural, and social science insights that can work together for our good as individuals, as families, and as a global Church.

CONCLUSION

We fully concur with and sustain President Nelson's prophetic vision and aims. We all have a river or two to cross before we reach the promised land; however, we hope that the wisdom that prophets and several exemplary families have shared will be helpful. Part of that vital wisdom is that spiritual experiences are essential, as discussed in the next chapter.

We conclude this chapter with a quote from Lisa Miller's book *The Spiritual Child*. Dr. Miller is a clinical psychologist and professor who has studied spirituality in children. She states the following:

> There is no question that the parenting journey wears away our ego, but ultimately we are not made less by the exhaustion, tired eyes, worn short-term memory, and endless laundry. Rather, we are so very much more—from our children's wondrous arrival into our lives to their

rounds of questioning and development, when we pay attention and we reflect, we can see great things through their spiritual lens.

What if this parenting journey is actually the ultimate spiritual journey? The equivalent to the deep awakening of the isolated monk, the pilgrimage to Mecca or Jerusalem, or the climb up Mount Everest? . . .

. . . A commitment by all of us to foster children's spirituality . . . can truly change our global culture.[34]

QUESTIONS TO ENCOURAGE CONTEMPLATION AND CONVERSATION

1. Given that it has now been two hundred years since the First Vision, why is now an ideal time for a major reemphasis on "home-centered, Church-supported" gospel learning, study, and worship of the Savior?

2. Why is it that individual study and worship combined with family study and worship have significantly more impact on deep conversion and behavior than either approach by itself? What are the implications and applications of this for you and your family?

3. How can you and your family strike a healthy balance between firmness and flexibility in your home-based religious practices? Do you tend to err in either direction? How might better harmony and balance be found?

4. Family researcher and therapist William J. Doherty has said, "The biggest threat to good marriages is everyday living."[35] How can engaging in individual, couple, and family worship and study in the home help protect us against the dangers of "everyday living"? What does your family do well? What would you like to do better?

5. Given that no family is perfect, why is it still of value to carefully consider the challenges, frustrations, trials, and successes of "exemplary" families? What are some vital lessons you have learned from observing "exemplary" individuals and families during your life? Have some (or many or most) of those exemplars been from outside The Church of Jesus Christ of Latter-day Saints? How can we better respond to President Nelson's invitation to become "exemplary Latter-day Saints"?

CREATING OPPORTUNITIES FOR REVELATORY EXPERIENCES (CORE)

1. What intentions do you have to enjoy personal revelatory experiences?
2. How can you and your loved ones encourage each other's revelatory experiences?
3. What personal and relational activities might encourage your own revelatory experiences?

NOTES

1. Quoted in "Latter-day Saint Prophet, Wife and Apostle Share Insights of Global Ministry," October 30, 2018, https://newsroom.ChurchofJesusChrist.org/article/latter-day-saint-prophet-wife-apostle-share-insights-global-ministry#churchofjesuschrist.
2. LeGrand R. Curtis Jr., "The Ongoing Restoration," *Ensign*, April 2020, 20–25.
3. Russell M. Nelson, "Revelation for the Church, Revelation for Our Lives," *Ensign*, May 2018, 95–96.
4. David A. Bednar, in "Panel Discussion" (worldwide leadership training meeting, November 2010), broadcasts.ChurchofJesusChrist.org.
5. David A. Bednar, "The Spirit of Revelation," *Ensign*, May 2011, 87.
6. Sydney Walker and Sarah Jane Weaver, "Inside Church Headquarters Photo Gallery: 17 Things We've Learned about Councils," *Church News*, updated August 5, 2021, https://www.thechurchnews.com/leaders-and-ministry/2021-08-05/inside-church-headquarters-photo-gallery-summary-points-220912.
7. *True to the Faith: A Gospel Reference* (Salt Lake City: The Church of Jesus Christ of Latter-day Saints, 2004), 140–41.
8. *Teachings of Presidents of the Church: Joseph Smith* (Salt Lake City: The Church of Jesus Christ of Latter-day Saints, 2007), 426.
9. Emphasis added. Every *Come, Follow Me—For Sunday School* manual published so far has included this instruction. See, for example, *Come, Follow Me—For Sunday School: Old Testament 2022*, xii.
10. For an insightful discussion of this divine-pattern idea, see Byran B. Korth, "Parents Teaching Children to Believe in Christ: 'An Echo of a Celestial Pattern,'" in *Give Ear to My Words: Text and Context of Alma 36–42*, ed. Kerry M. Hull, Nicholas J. Frederick, and Hank R. Smith (Provo, UT: Religious Studies Center, Brigham Young University; Salt Lake City: Deseret Book, 2019), 341–68.
11. Russell M. Nelson, "Opening Remarks," *Ensign*, November 2018, 7.
12. Nelson, "Opening Remarks," 7–8.
13. D. Todd Christofferson, "Why the Church," *Ensign*, November 2015, 108, 110.
14. J. E. McCulloch, *Home: The Savior of Civilization* (Washington, DC: Southern Co-operative League, 1924), 42.
15. Nelson, "Opening Remarks," 8. In note 2, President Nelson referenced the Lord's words in Doctrine and Covenants 93:40 ("I have commanded you to bring up your children in light and truth") and in Moses 6:58–62 ("to teach these things freely unto your children, . . . the plan of salvation").
16. Nelson, "Opening Remarks," 8.

17. Quentin L. Cook, "Deep and Lasting Conversion to Heavenly Father and the Lord Jesus Christ," *Ensign*, November 2018, 10.
18. Brent L. Top and Bruce A. Chadwick, *Rearing Righteous Youth of Zion* (Salt Lake City: Bookcraft, 1998), 87; emphasis in original.
19. Top and Chadwick, *Rearing Righteous Youth of Zion*, 87.
20. Cook, "Deep and Lasting Conversion," 10.
21. Cook, "Deep and Lasting Conversion," 11.
22. The repeated uses of the word "conversion" were modified or contextualized as follows: (1) "deepening conversion," (2) "deepening individual conversion," (3) "the Spirit increases and strengthens conversion," (4) "deep and lasting conversion" (four times), (5) "deepening conversion to Heavenly Father and the Lord Jesus Christ," (6) "deepen our conversion," and (7) "true conversion."
23. Cook, "Deep and Lasting Conversion," 11.
24. See David C. Dollahite et al., "Beyond Religious Rigidities: Religious Firmness and Religious Flexibility as Complementary Loyalties in Faith Transmission," *Religions* 10, no. 2 (2019): 111.
25. D. Todd Christofferson, "Why Marriage, Why Family," *Ensign*, May 2015, 52.
26. Russell M. Nelson, "Becoming Exemplary Latter-day Saints," *Ensign*, November 2018, 113.
27. See David C. Dollahite and Loren D. Marks, eds., *Strengths in Diverse Families of Faith: Exploring Religious Differences* (New York: Routledge, 2020).
28. See David C. Dollahite and Jennifer Y. Thatcher, "Talking about Religion: How Highly Religious Youth and Parents Discuss Their Faith," *Journal of Adolescent Research* 23, no. 5 (2008): 611–41.
29. See William J. Doherty, *Take Back Your Marriage: Sticking Together in a World That Pulls Us Apart* (New York: Guilford, 2001), 125.
30. Nelson, "Becoming Exemplary Latter-day Saints," 114.
31. See Dollahite et al., "Beyond Religious Rigidities."
32. See Naomi W. Randall, "I Am a Child of God," in *Hymns* (Salt Lake City: The Church of Jesus Christ of Latter-day Saints, 1985), no. 301.
33. Dieter F. Uchtdorf, "The Love of God," *Ensign*, November 2009, 21.
34. Lisa Miller, *The Spiritual Child* (New York: Picador, 2015), 19–20; emphasis added.
35. Doherty, *Take Back Your Marriage*, 125.

CHAPTER TWO

Personal and Shared Revelatory Experiences

In this chapter we focus on revelatory experiences in the home and how to facilitate them for various family members. As in chapter 1, we explore insights from the scriptures, from President Nelson and other modern prophets, and from social science research interviews and surveys we have conducted with individual members and families from around the United States. Again, our aim is to highlight and celebrate both personal and familial worship efforts designed to connect us with and more deeply convert us to the Eternal Father and His Son, Jesus Christ, through the Holy Ghost.

INSIGHTS FROM THE SCRIPTURES

As discussed in the previous chapter, the process of parents communing with God and then teaching their children has been present from the beginning. Indeed, it is so prevalent in Adam and Eve's story in the scriptures that we would like to say a little more about it. Exploring the example of Adam and Eve as recorded in the first twelve verses of Moses 5 is instructive. Verse 1 tells us that Adam and Eve labored *together* in supplying life's necessities by tilling the earth. Verses 2–3 report that Eve and Adam bore children who, in turn, bore children of their own. So our first parents were also our first grandparents.

In verse 4 we learn that "*Adam and Eve*, his wife, called upon the name of the Lord, and *they* heard the voice of the Lord . . . speaking unto *them*" (Moses 5:4; emphasis added). We find this verse particularly interesting and instructive since the use of *them* informs us that the first recorded human communion with the Lord following the Fall and expulsion from the Garden of Eden was a *shared revelatory experience*.

The next verse tells us that God "gave unto *them* commandments, that *they* should worship the Lord *their* God, and should offer the firstlings of *their* flocks, for an offering unto the Lord" (Moses 5:5; emphasis added). Again, the repeated use of plural pronouns ("them," "they," "their") makes it clear that the Lord was in a sacred revelatory relationship with both our first parents (and first grandparents) and that they were having shared revelatory experiences from the beginning.

Moses 5:6–8 records that, as commanded, Adam built an altar, offered sacrifices, and then experienced an angelic visitation. Next, verse 9 tells of a personal revelatory experience when the Holy Ghost bore record to Adam of the Father and the Son and the Redemption. Verse 10 tells us that "in that day Adam blessed God and was filled" (presumably with the Holy Ghost) and that he prophesied "concerning all the families of the earth" about the blessings that came from the Fall, his love of God, his joy in the gospel, and his hope of seeing God in the flesh. Verse 11 records that Eve "heard all these things and was glad," and then she also spoke of the blessings of the Fall—having seed, knowing good and evil, the joy of "our" redemption, and eternal life. The next verse tells us that "Adam and Eve blessed the name of God, and *they* made all things known unto their sons and their daughters" (verse 12; emphasis added).

As parents and grandparents in the last days, we can learn much from the first twelve verses in Moses 5. Together Eve and Adam had profound shared sacred encounters with the Father, the Son, and the Holy Ghost. They also had personal revelatory experiences that they soon shared with each other. They rejoiced together in the Lord and in the doctrine of redemption they received. They shared their experiences with their posterity, and they recorded their sacred revelatory experiences so that "all the families of the earth" could know about their first parents and their sacred encounters with the Lord. Adam and Eve were clearly equal and active partners in seeking to commune with God, to share their personal sacred experiences with each other, and to share those revelatory experiences together with their posterity.

Another scriptural account that addresses shared revelation as well as deep and lasting conversion in a home and family setting is offered by the experiences of many men, women, and children during King Benjamin's address at the temple. While chapters 2–5 of Mosiah include marvelous doctrine about a range of issues, here we focus on those verses that tell of the *shared* spiritual experience enjoyed by many Saints: "And it came to pass that when they came up to the temple, they pitched their tents round about, every man according to his family, consisting of his wife, and his sons, and his daughters, and their sons, and their daughters, from the eldest down to the youngest, every family being separate one from another" (Mosiah 2:5).

Note that each extended family was in a tent (some tents must have been quite large) and that every family was gathered separately. "And they pitched their tents round about the temple, every man having his tent with the door thereof towards the temple, that thereby they might remain in their tents and hear the words which king Benjamin should speak unto them" (Mosiah 2:6). The fact that each family gathered together to hear the words of their prophet-king fits with the profound gospel doctrine that families are the fundamental unit of eternity and of the Church of Jesus Christ. Note that each family arranged their tent so that the door faced the temple, allowing them to view the house of the Lord and to hear the word of the Lord. One way to understand this spatial ordering is that families can strive to arrange and literally orient themselves in ways that open them up to things sacred, including sacred revelatory experiences.

King Benjamin gave a timeless address in which he repeated the words of an angel whose message centered on the life and atoning sacrifice of Jesus Christ. Following his address, King Benjamin noticed that all the people had fallen to the earth (see Mosiah 4:1). The reason for this fear and submissive prostration to the earth was then recorded:

> And they had viewed themselves in their own carnal state, even less than the dust of the earth. And they all cried aloud with one voice, saying: O have mercy, and apply the atoning blood of Christ that *we* may receive forgiveness of our sins, and *our* hearts may be purified; for *we* believe in Jesus Christ, the Son of God, who created heaven and earth, and all things. . . .
>
> And it came to pass that after *they* had spoken these words *the Spirit of the Lord came upon them, and they were filled with joy, having received a remission of their sins, and having peace of conscience*, because of the exceeding faith which *they* had in Jesus Christ who should come, according to the words which king Benjamin had spoken unto *them*. (Mosiah 4:2–3; emphasis added)

After they had heard or read the words of the angel reported by King Benjamin, a spiritual outpouring occurred. Mosiah attributed this conversion to "the exceeding faith which they had in Jesus Christ" (verse 3). Mosiah chapter 5 provides more information about the conversion experienced by all those who heard or read King Benjamin's words:

> And *they all* cried with one voice, saying: Yea, *we* believe all the words which thou hast spoken unto *us*; and also, *we* know of their surety and truth, *because of the Spirit of the Lord Omnipotent, which has wrought a mighty change in us, or in our hearts, that we have no more disposition to do evil, but to do good continually*. . . .
>
> And it is the faith which *we* have had on the things which *our* king has spoken unto us that has brought *us* to this great knowledge, whereby *we* do rejoice with such exceedingly great joy. (Verses 2, 4; emphasis added)

In the two previous extended quotes from Mosiah, we used italics to emphasize (a) the plural pronouns and (b) the portions of the verses that mention the transcendent spiritual experiences the congregation had. This sacred revelatory experience was both *personal* and *shared* in a family context. It was personal because each person felt the love and power of God in his or her own mind, heart, and spirit. It was shared because these people were together in the same place and time when the Spirit was poured out on them all.

The shared experience enabled the listeners to know that what they personally experienced was not imagined or a purely personal experience but rather a profound, powerful, and eternally significant shared revelatory experience. They then knew for themselves that God lived, knew them, and could fill their souls with His love and mercy. This kind of personal transformative spiritual experience is the birthright of every person throughout history, across cultures and languages. It is a pearl of great price to be sought and treasured.

Likewise, in homes individuals can have personal sacred experiences, and families can experience the power of God's love together. The Savior's words "For where two or three are gathered together in my name, there am I in the midst of them" (Matthew 18:20) can be understood in the context of any gathering of disciples of Christ, including in homes, temples, chapels, and classrooms.

INSIGHTS ON REVELATORY EXPERIENCES FROM PROPHETS AND APOSTLES

Near the end of his life, the Prophet Joseph Smith stated, "I don't blame anyone for not believing my history. If I had not experienced what I have, I could not have believed it myself."[1] Joseph Smith was a person whose prayer of faith opened the heavens. If someone with such strong faith could admit that his story sounded unbelievable, then we should be very careful about what we expect others, including our children, to believe without the benefit of personal spiritual experiences of their own.

Note that Joseph said he "could not" (rather than "would not") have believed it. Perhaps Joseph needed the kind of proof that can come only from personal experience. In some ways, personal spiritual experience is the ultimate form of evidence. In the words of Joseph, "I had seen a vision; I knew it, and I knew that God knew it, and I could not deny it" (Joseph Smith—History 1:25).

While many of Joseph's revelatory experiences were given when Joseph was alone (for example, the First Vision and the appearances of Moroni), many were given in the presence of others, oftentimes scribes, and there were times when others shared the revelatory experience with him, such as the vision of the three degrees of glory shared with Sidney Rigdon (see Doctrine and Covenants 76). These examples suggest how important it is to structure our family life—especially the religious aspects—in ways that are more likely to facilitate family members having spiritual experiences that can lead to deep and lasting conversion.

In an April 2021 general conference address, President Nelson stated, "To do anything well requires effort. Becoming a true disciple of Jesus Christ is no exception. Increasing your faith and trust in Him takes effort. . . . Faith takes work. Receiving revelation takes work."[2] The veil that separates us from the realities all around us may be pierced with a combination of faith in higher things, intellectual and spiritual humility, obedience to eternal laws, purity of heart, patience and long-suffering, and patterned spiritual practice that is unique to each person, place, and time. The lasting blessings that accompany opening the door to the Savior, inviting the presence of the Holy Ghost, and receiving knowledge of eternal realities from our Father are worth the required effort. Obtaining a knowledge of truth is personally expensive—it costs us sacrifice, effort, and obedience (see John 7:17). Truth is not called the pearl of small price.

Parents, grandparents, and other family members can assist family members by facilitating the blessing of personal and interpersonal revelatory experiences that contribute to personal conversion. When family members (a) seek their own personal revelatory experiences, (b) share those experiences with family members, and (c) take time together to seek revelatory experiences, lasting personal conversion is more likely to occur.

In one of his first general conference addresses to the Saints after being sustained as prophet, seer, and revelator, President Russell M. Nelson emphasized the importance of personal, spiritual, and revelatory experience:

> One of the things the Spirit has repeatedly impressed upon my mind since my new calling as President of the Church is how willing the Lord is to reveal His mind and will. The privilege of receiving revelation is one of the greatest gifts of God to His children. . . .
>
> Pray in the name of Jesus Christ about your concerns, your fears, your weaknesses—yes, the very longings of your heart. . . .

> . . . In coming days, it will not be possible to survive spiritually without the guiding, directing, comforting, and constant influence of the Holy Ghost.[3]

President Nelson's teaching about spiritual survival in "coming days" is consistent with words spoken by Elder Heber C. Kimball:

> To meet the difficulties that are coming, it will be necessary for you to have a knowledge of the truth of this work for yourselves. The difficulties will be of such a character that the man or woman who does not possess this personal knowledge or witness will fall. If you have not got the testimony, live right and call upon the Lord and cease not till you obtain it. If you do not you will not stand. . . . The time will come when no man nor woman will be able to endure on borrowed light.[4]

One experience with the Spirit will not be enough—we need the constant influence of the Holy Ghost. In a later conference talk, President Russell M. Nelson said, "For many years, Church leaders have been working on an integrated curriculum to strengthen families and individuals through a *home-centered* and *Church-supported* plan to learn doctrine, strengthen faith, and foster greater personal worship."[5] President Nelson's three stated purposes for this plan and curriculum were to (1) learn doctrine, (2) strengthen faith, and (3) foster greater personal worship.

In an address titled "Come, Follow Me," President Nelson specifically emphasized the need for personal experiences with God: "Put yourself in a position to begin having experiences with Him. Humble yourself. Pray to have eyes to see God's hand in your life and in the world around you. Ask Him to tell you if He is really there—if He knows you. Ask Him how He feels about you. And then listen."[6]

In his book *The Spirit of Revelation*, Elder David A. Bednar taught important principles about a shared process of experiencing revelation:

> A fundamental principle of revelation is that it is "scattered among us." As we participate in a ward or family council, everyone in that council is responsible to be "anxiously engaged" (Doctrine and Covenants

58:27), share impressions from the Spirit, and contribute to a *shared revelatory process*. If individuals feel safe and can give voice to some of their questions, concerns, and uncertainties in a class, in a family, in a council meeting, and in a variety of other settings, then they participate in *a collective expression of faith* in the Lord Jesus Christ that invites and entices the Holy Ghost to be the teacher.[7]

Among the "variety of other settings" that can result in what Elder Bednar calls a "shared revelatory process" are family gatherings such as family prayer, home evening, family scripture study, and family mealtimes. When family members "share impressions from the Spirit" and "contribute to a shared revelatory process," they are engaging in revelatory and relational processes that can bless individuals, couples, and families with the sweet "fruit of the Spirit" that the Apostle Paul said included "love, joy, peace, longsuffering, gentleness, goodness, faith, meekness, [and] temperance" (Galatians 5:22–23).

In an "Evening with a General Authority" online training session for Latter-day Saints involved in the Church Educational System (CES), Elder Bednar emphasized that all Latter-day Saints who have been confirmed and are trying to keep their covenants "are living in revelation." That is because those who have received the gift of the Holy Ghost are promised that the Spirit will be a "constant companion" if they keep their covenants and that they can "always have [the] Spirit to be with [them]."[8] He stressed that while people tend to think that they need to do something special or follow some formulaic behaviors to get ready to receive revelation, they would be better served by remembering that revelation is being poured out on them continually and that they can constantly be in revelation.

Based on these recent apostolic teachings, we use Elder Bednar's phrase "revelatory experience"[9] to refer to those times when *we more fully recognize that we are receiving revelation* rather than to all times when we are receiving revelation. In other words, since revelation is always available to us and is always being poured out on us, revelatory experiences are when we become more aware of that constant revelation. For us, Elder Bednar's teachings harmonize beautifully with the Savior's words to His ancient disciples that "lo, I am with you alway" (Matthew 28:20) and with His words to His disciples in 1832:

The light shineth in darkness, and the darkness comprehendeth it not; nevertheless, the day shall come when you shall comprehend even God, being quickened in him and by him.

Then shall ye know that ye have seen me, that I am, and that I am the true light that is in you, and that you are in me; otherwise ye could not abound. (Doctrine and Covenants 88:49–50)

ETERNAL FAMILIES DESERVE SHARED REVELATORY EXPERIENCES

In the 150th Semiannual General Conference of the Church, President Spencer W. Kimball said,

> From the beginning, The Church of Jesus Christ of Latter-day Saints has emphasized family life. We have always understood that the foundations of the family, as an eternal unit, were laid even before this earth was created! . . .
>
> Oh, brothers and sisters, *families can be forever!* Do not let the lures of the moment draw you away from them! *Divinity, eternity,* and *family*—they go together, hand in hand, and so must we![10]

Additionally, the *Gospel Principles* manual teaches that "the family is the most important unit in The Church of Jesus Christ of Latter-day Saints. The Church exists to help families gain eternal blessings and exaltation. The organizations and programs within the Church are designed to strengthen us individually and help us live as families forever."[11]

Mention of "eternal blessings" and living as "families forever" points to the holy temples that offer these transcendent blessings. Of the temple, the Bible Dictionary states, "It is the most holy of any place of worship on the earth. Only the home can compare with the temple in sacredness."[12] Temples and homes are sacred for several reasons, but one vital reason is that they are places where revelatory experiences can occur for individuals and families. President Russell M. Nelson stated, "We hope and pray that each member's home will become a true sanctuary of faith, where the Spirit of the Lord may dwell. Despite contention all around us, one's home can become a heavenly place, where study, prayer, and faith can be merged with love."[13] When individuals and families strive for their homes to become sanctuaries of faith, the Lord can pour out personal and interpersonal revelatory experiences that will bless them and help them be a blessing to other families.

SPIRITUAL FIRES AND PERSONAL CONVERSION

In one account of the First Vision, Joseph describes not only "a pillar of light" but also "fire," although "nothing consumed."[14] In a *BYU Studies Quarterly* article discussing Joseph's accounts of his First Vision, Professor Kathleen Flake reported,

> All four of the . . . accounts of his first vision convey sense impression, not merely words or mental impressions. They emphasize his having seen a great light, as great as and even brighter than the sun at "noon day" and as a "pillar of flame which was spread all around." The light "rested upon" him and bathed the world in a fire that did not burn, but "filled [him] with the spirit of god." . . . When the pillar of light or flame appeared, it expelled the darkness.[15]

Joseph's experience bears similarities to another fire witnessed millennia earlier by Moses. For both prophets, the experience of the fire or burning ignited the beginnings of a new life, a deepened personal faith that inspired millions of others. President Joseph F. Smith said:

> By the whisperings of the still small voice of the spirit of the living God, He gave to me the testimony I possess. And by this principle and power He will give to all the children of men a knowledge of the truth that will stay with them, and it will make them to know the truth, as God knows it, and to do the will of the Father as Christ does it. And no amount of marvelous manifestations will ever accomplish this.[16]

SOCIAL SCIENCE SUPPORT FOR SCRIPTURAL TRUTHS

We now shift from sacred to social experience and research. Anthropologist Barbara Myerhoff not only studied but experienced and immersed herself in the lives of aging Jews for the last decade of her life before cancer prevailed. Myerhoff offered the summative wisdom she gained in a volume titled *Number Our Days* and included the following narrative from a Jewish man named Shmuel, who explained to her,

> When the great Hasid[ic leader], Baal Shem Tov, the Master of the Good Name, had a problem, it was his custom to go to a certain part of the forest. There he would light a fire and say a certain prayer, and find wisdom. A generation later, a son of one of his disciples was in the same position. He went to that same place in the forest and lit the fire, but he could not remember the prayer. But he asked for wisdom and it was sufficient. He found what he needed. A generation after that, his son had a problem like the others. He also went to the forest, but he could not even light the fire. "Lord of the Universe," he prayed, "I [can]not remember the prayer and I cannot get the fire started. But I am in the forest. That will have to be sufficient."[17]

In Shmuel's report each generation loses something. Reading this three-generation tale reminds us of Jeffrey R. Holland's haunting statement: "This Church is always one generation away from extinction."[18] Perhaps each generation, even each member, needs its own revelatory experience with the "fire in the forest," or else a day will come when the hopes, prayers, and fire from the previous generations will not "be sufficient."

Indeed, one vital consideration in deepening conversion and strengthening faith is personal spiritual experience. If a person only hears about other people's experiences of a "burning bush," the "Spirit of God" burning "like a fire,"[19] or a spiritual fire in a sacred grove but does not personally experience the warmth and light of revelation from God, he or she may not be fully converted. Hebrews 12:29 states, "For our God is a consuming fire." Personal experience with the love and power of God can consume our sense of profound spiritual loneliness, our own personal sins and weakness, and our lack of purpose.

Support for this idea comes from social science. In Jana Riess's recent book-length study focused on millennials who are (or were) members of The Church of Jesus Christ of Latter-day Saints, Riess notes the shared features of millennials who continue to identify as Latter-day Saints:

> The successful transmission of a religious identity is based on a combination of three indispensable elements: orthodox belief, an accepted code of behavior, and . . . *transformative religious experience.* This third category is paramount if rising generations are to fully inhabit the faith of their parents. In other words, the "secret sauce" of religion as a core identity has to include not just the shoulds and shouldn'ts of belief and behavior, but also a palpable sense that a devotee has *personally encountered the divine.*[20]

The kind of "transformative religious experience" that Reiss refers to in which someone "has personally encountered the divine" is crucial to initial and deepening conversion. We find it fascinating that prophetic teaching, social science research, and scriptural accounts all seem to point to the importance of parents having revelatory experiences, sharing those experiences with the next generation, and facilitating ways for their children and grandchildren to have their own personal and shared revelatory experiences.

We believe the principles and practices explored in this book can help both parents and grandparents consider ways they can encourage and facilitate personal and interpersonal revelatory experiences among their children and grandchildren. Elder Bednar taught, "If members of families, as they come together, would think in terms of 'I'm preparing to participate in a revelatory experience with my family' . . . I think we would prepare and act much differently."[21] When an Apostle of the Lord suggests that family members prepare and act *much* differently, it suggests he is inviting more than minor tweaks in current practices. We believe that parents and grandparents can and should counsel together and seek inspiration about how they might better prepare for and act in regular family gatherings in ways that are more likely to facilitate personal and interpersonal revelatory experiences. When one feels the power and influence of the Holy Ghost, one learns of realities beyond what can only be seen with physical eyes, heard with physical ears, or felt with mortal flesh.

This feeling of personally encountering the divine and developing a deep "relationship with God" is supported by many of the diverse but faithful persons we have interviewed in depth. Aisha,[22] a Muslim mother, said:

There is one thing that I want to say to people: "Let no man get between you and God." Your relationship with God is so important, we shouldn't let anyone hold us back—not even friends, or a husband, or a sister or brother. . . . We get stuff in our own time. We walk at a different pace. We can't be looking at people who are not as far along as us and judge them. They've got to come at their own pace. However, I need to make sure nothing gets between me and God.

Similarly, an African Methodist father named Rashaad said, "I just want to say that God is real. He's not a figment of your imagination. He's real. . . . He lives . . . and we're all God's children."

Rashaad's point was reiterated and expounded on by a Christian mother who said,

God is someone who is alive and real and wants to be a part of our life, not just an abstract idea but a person—a person who is interested in us and who knows us and loves us and wants us to be in a relationship with Him. When you get to that point, when you realize that He cares about you as a person and that He's real, someone who's here even though we can't see Him—[when you grasp] the reality of Him loving us beyond what we can now understand—that is the beginning [of a different kind of life].

SPIRITUAL EXPERIENCES: INSIGHTS FROM THE HOMES OF FAITHFUL FAMILIES

Many of the families of diverse faiths that we interviewed allowed us onto their "sacred ground" and shared spiritual experiences that made a difference in their family relationships. For many families, spiritual or even transcendent experiences during challenges reportedly offered deeper meaning not only in family relationships but also in their relationships with God. A Latter-day Saint husband and father named Jake said:

Having kids and becoming a father has helped me understand what my Heavenly Father must feel and go through watching me. You . . . would do everything for your kids if you could . . . [but] there are times that you can't . . . and [they need to] learn from experience. . . . When [my son] was sick, I felt how our Heavenly Father must feel whenever one of us is sick. . . . It's . . . made me appreciate what being a loving father is like. It's made me appreciate that aspect of God as a father and the sacrifice He made for His Son to come to earth. I can't imagine what that was like.

Sometimes spiritual experiences during adversity might appropriately be called "the refiner's fire." Such experiences, though painful, sometimes deepened family relationships, as reported by Hal, a Latter-day Saint father of a prematurely born child:

> It was certainly a . . . humbling experience . . . to realize that no matter what we do, it [could be God's] will . . . that [our] baby may not live. . . . [Knowing] there was a greater power who was . . . mindful and underst[anding] helped me to just trust . . . that even if our baby died, that was not the end, that we [would] see the baby again. . . . Looking back, I am grateful for that. It made me a stronger person. . . . It made our family stronger.

When her husband was near death, a Latter-day Saint woman named Lynette recalled,

> I just remember sitting there in the hospital room thinking, "I'm too young to be a widow." . . . [The bishop] . . . showed up, and . . . I literally saw the power of heaven descend. I tell you, it was just amazing. . . . I think it made us stronger together and just really made us appreciate life a lot more.

Another Latter-day Saint parent, following the loss of a child, said, "It was . . . an experience that . . . really strengthened our faith and . . . brought us closer together."

For many diverse but exemplary families we have interviewed, times of greatest trial sometimes yielded the deepest spiritual experiences. Faith often enabled individuals and families to navigate trials and profound challenges in ways that strengthened rather than weakened them. Similarly, Alma 62:41 mentions both hardening and softening in response to war:

> But behold, because of the exceedingly great length of the war between the Nephites and the Lamanites many had become hardened, . . . and many were softened because of their afflictions, insomuch that they did humble themselves before God, even in the depth of humility.

It appears that when faced with adversity, we can choose to humble ourselves and turn to God for succor. We can choose to "look to God and live" (Alma 37:47), since, as King Lamoni taught, "[the Lord] has given us a portion of his Spirit to soften our hearts" (Alma 24:8). Elder Neal A. Maxwell taught, "Partaking of a bitter cup without becoming bitter is . . . part of the emulation of Jesus."[23]

Spiritual experiences also came in ordinary settings. Other relational actions—smaller, everyday decisions—were also framed in sacred language by the diverse families we interviewed. One Latter-day Saint woman's spiritual experience moved her to see her husband as God "saw him":

> [I had this strong feeling that] I had to be patient and try not to be too judgmental . . . to see him again the way that Heavenly Father saw him, . . . that Heavenly Father was very pleased with the efforts that he was making, was happy that [my husband] was trying to make the right decisions, and He didn't expect him to be perfect from the beginning. The Savior taught us to love each other as we love ourselves and to be kind to each other, to be charitable. That has been an important part of our marriage, to try to follow these teachings.

Another spiritual and relational experience stimulated by the hassles of the "everyday" was shared with us by a young Latter-day Saint mother named Rachel:[24]

> I was a mother of three young children, living in a five-hundred-square-foot apartment in a new city, my husband working an accountant's busy season during a dark, cold winter. All three children were home

with me all day every day for the time being, as we homeschooled kindergarten and preschool and chased a toddler. I love my work as a mother, but during this season I was fatigued and found my patience strained—especially around bedtime.

I stuck to a strict bedtime routine of PJs, teeth, toilet, a story, prayer, a lullaby, and in bed by 7:00. At that point in the day, even the best day, I was done—worn out physically, mentally, spiritually. I needed to shut the kids' bedroom door, pull out the Ben & Jerry's, and block out anything "kid." And that's what I did for a while. After all, I'd done all the things a "good mom" was supposed to do all during the day.

But the children continually snuck out of bed with excuses. All the usual ones: drinks of water, bathroom, to see what I was reading or watching. "Why can't I have ice cream too? Where is Daddy? When will Daddy come home? I'm bored. I'm scared. I'm not tired."

Things continued to get harder that winter, particularly with one child. I could feel the tension between us building to the point of blowing up. I began to earnestly seek a solution to the stress of that last part of the day, sensing it set the tone for a lot of the feeling in our home. I read blog articles, and Google told me I was already doing all the "right" things to set up bedtime to be successful.

One evening I had a thought to read a time when Jesus loved the children. I opened to 3 Nephi, looking for the time when Jesus blessed the little children and angels surrounded them. I've always loved that part. As I was scanning the pages, my eyes alighted on a section that seemed to be marked, though there was no red underlining. I read where Jesus had been with the people all day, teaching and ministering. He announced that it was time for Him to go, but He would return the next day. As He was about to leave, the people began to cry. They looked at Him "as if they would ask him to tarry a little longer with them" [3 Nephi 17:5]. He looked at them, and He was moved with compassion. He told them to bring all their afflictions to Him, and He would heal them in His mercy.

The Spirit, who had highlighted those verses for me, sunk deep into my heart the answer to my question of how I needed to mother beyond the 100 percent I was already giving. My children were begging me to "tarry a little longer," and I needed to give just a little more. It seemed like a big ask at that time, when I was so weary. The Spirit had never steered me wrong before, so I had to trust that this example of Christ's was one I must follow.

The next night I put the children to bed as usual and told them I would be back in ten minutes to talk to them each individually. I returned after a short shake-off of the day. I knelt by each bedside in turn. There I took a few minutes to call the child by name, stroke their hair, chat about the day, pray with, and give an extra-long hug to.

As I continued this for a few nights, then weeks in a row, I noticed a change in the mood during the evenings. There w[ere] less whining and fussing delays during the bedtime routine. The children didn't need to come out as much after the extra few minutes I spent with them. Most importantly, I noticed that during the day my relationship with the child who needed me most was improving. We had more patience for each other.

The Spirit guided me to the right place at the right time for the benefit of all the children in our house—me as well as my little ones.

Rachel's experience of being moved and instructed as a young mother by the Savior's actions in 3 Nephi to "tarry a little longer" with her children seems to embody the counsel of President Nelson when he said, "Make time to study His words. Really study! If you truly love your family and if you desire to be exalted with them throughout eternity, pay the price now—through serious study and fervent prayer—to know these eternal truths and then to abide by them."[25] Rachel studied, prayed, received the truth she needed, and then strove "to abide by" that truth.

Camilla,[26] a Latter-day Saint single adult in her thirties, recalled a spiritual experience that was familial in context. Speaking of sacred moments, she said,

The experience that sprang directly to mind is from one particular family home evening. I remember sitting on the couch, each member of my family all around me in the seats they always sat in, the piano across the room. The wooden armrest of the couch was worn smooth. I don't remember if we were singing or reading or discussing, but I remember the feeling of hollowness in the pit of my stomach, tightness in my chest, and loss. It took me a few minutes to identify the feeling—I was homesick. When I realized what I was feeling, I was confused. How could I be homesick when I was literally at home, surrounded by my family? A thought came to my mind that I was homesick for heaven. I was safe and loved and surrounded by family, and that was what heaven was like.

While on this earth, we are all, like Abraham, a stranger in a strange land. At times, especially times when we feel the Spirit most strongly, and thus when the veil between heaven and earth is particularly thin, we can feel even more out of place here in this mortal existence. When our heavenly home beckons to us in the midst of our own happy earthly home, we can share with our fellow family members that we are all on a sacred, eternal journey back to our heavenly home and encourage each family member to try to be helpful to each other along this covenant path.

As we reflect on the small collection of revelatory experiences recounted above, we see that some are personal and some involve other people; some arise from profound challenges, and some arise from the everyday or mundane; some involve formal worship, study, or prayer, while others emerge from the rhythm of life. Each of these accounts reflects an interpersonal revelatory experience in the sense that the person was willing to open up and share deeply personal sacred experiences with the person he or she was speaking or writing to. Perhaps opportunities to find the fire of "deep and lasting conversion" are available in an array of life experiences. One of our BYU students recently wrote in an assignment,

> I was raised in a highly religious environment, and "rigid" is a good way to describe the way religion was carried out in the home. Since my siblings and I are now grown, it is difficult to watch as two of my brothers struggle with the teachings of the gospel and following the

Savior in their lives. I know my parents were trying their best with the knowledge and understanding they had, and it is unfortunate that the outcomes have been less than perfect. I want to learn from past mistakes and ensure that my future family improves on what I experienced in my childhood. . . . In the article [we read for class], one particular mother expressed her concerns with teaching her children and the pressure she felt with that responsibility. She then expressed, "*The mistake I have made in the past is trying to teach something that has to be experienced*," and my thoughts began to understand a missing link my parents demonstrated. They had come to know through experiences and feelings that the gospel of Jesus Christ is real and true, and instead of ensuring their children had those same feelings, they got caught up in the preaching and teaching.

In essence, there was a lack of experience with the Spirit. That experience with the Spirit is the true beauty of the gospel. The basics of the gospel, such as family prayer, scripture study, and family home evening are important habits to form, but if children are not leaving those sacred moments feeling and experiencing something with the Divine, then those practices could be a waste of time. I would daresay those parents could have been better off not to have the rigid discourse in the first place. . . . I want to create a legacy of consistency and obedience with my family.

However, I hope to remember that it is not necessarily the lengthy sermons or the specific wording that is being taught, but the importance resides in what is going on in the heart of my children. I think this can be achieved when short, powerful messages are shared and as the Spirit has the opportunity to come into their hearts. Potential ways to help children feel and experience could be to ask questions such as "What are you feeling? How does knowing Jesus loves you make you feel?" I think it is a blessing to listen as sweet children of God begin to articulate what it is like to experience the gospel rather than simply learn about it.

Reflecting on these revelatory experiences from a diverse array of individuals in varied life circumstances, we note the following commonalities:

1. Focusing on relationships helped yield personal revelatory experiences by providing extra motivation to receive revelation, insights into who God is, and motivation to repent and restore harmony after family conflict.
2. Faith often enabled individuals and families to navigate trials in a way that strengthened them rather than weakened them. Successfully enduring challenges together often yielded both personal and family revelatory experiences by giving families a reason to rally together and rely on the Lord.
3. Personal and family revelatory experiences often brought strengthened family relationships.[27]

Joseph Smith found the fire of the Spirit in the forest. He experienced the gospel as well as a relationship with Him who is the Giver of the Gospel. In the next chapter, we will see that faithful personal study and worship are among the most important ways that we can put ourselves in optimal position to begin having our own experiences with the unquenchable flame, the Light of the World.

QUESTIONS TO ENCOURAGE CONTEMPLATION AND CONVERSATION

1. When have you "experienced" God, and how can you facilitate such experiences again? How can you help your family members and loved ones desire to have similar revelatory experiences?
2. There are many ways that we may experience personalized versions of "the fire in the forest," such as worshipping in the temple, serving others, engaging in deep study and prayer, and witnessing births. What are your approaches? How do you keep the fire alive?
3. Have there been times when you have experienced the refiner's fire? How did you change? Have you maintained or built upon those changes?
4. Like Rachel, the young mother who was impressed to "tarry a little longer with [her children]," have there been everyday or mundane challenges in your life that have led to rich spiritual experiences? If so, have you recorded them and shared them with your family?

CREATING OPPORTUNITIES FOR REVELATORY EXPERIENCES (CORE)

1. What intentions do you have to enjoy personal revelatory experiences?
2. How can you and your loved ones encourage each other's revelatory experiences?
3. What personal and relational activities might encourage your own revelatory experiences?

NOTES

1. Joseph Smith, "History, 1838–1856, volume E-1 [1 July 1843–30 April 1844]," p. 1979, The Joseph Smith Papers, https://www.josephsmithpapers.org/paper-summary/history-1838-1856-volume-e-1-1-july-1843-30-april-1844/351.
2. Russell M. Nelson, "Christ Is Risen; Faith in Him Will Move Mountains," *Liahona*, May 2021, 103.
3. Russell M. Nelson, "Revelation for the Church, Revelation for Our Lives," *Ensign*, May 2018, 94, 96.
4. Quoted in Orson F. Whitney, *Life of Heber C. Kimball* (Salt Lake City: Bookcraft, 1967), 450.
5. Russell M. Nelson, "Opening Remarks," *Ensign*, November 2018, 8; emphasis in original.
6. Russell M. Nelson, "Come, Follow Me," *Ensign*, May 2019, 90.
7. David A. Bednar, *The Spirit of Revelation* (Salt Lake City: Deseret Book, 2021), 58; emphasis added.
8. David A. Bednar, in "An Evening with a General Authority—David A. Bednar Discussion," Called to Share, April 10, 2020, YouTube video, https://www.youtube.com/watch?v=vGfGtYFZ6jA.
9. David A. Bednar, in "Panel Discussion" (worldwide leadership training meeting, November 2010), broadcasts.ChurchofJesusChrist.org.
10. Spencer W. Kimball, "Families Can Be Eternal," *Ensign*, November 1980, 4, 5; emphasis in original.
11. *Gospel Principles* (Salt Lake City: The Church of Jesus Christ of Latter-day Saints, 2009), 36.
12. Bible Dictionary, "Temple."
13. Russell M. Nelson, "Closing Remarks," *Ensign*, May 2019, 111.
14. Steven C. Harper, *Joseph Smith's First Vision: A Guide to the Historical Accounts* (Salt Lake City: Deseret Book, 2012).
15. Kathleen Flake, "The First Vision as a Prehistory of The Church of Jesus Christ of Latter-day Saints," *BYU Studies Quarterly* 59, no. 2 (2020): 59–72.
16. Joseph F. Smith, in Conference Report, April 1900, 40–41.
17. Barbara Myerhoff, *Number Our Days* (New York: Meridian, 1979), 112.
18. Jeffrey R. Holland, "That Our Children May Know" (Brigham Young University devotional, August 25, 1981), 4, https://speeches.byu.edu/talks/jeffrey-r-holland/children-may-know/.
19. William W. Phelps, "The Spirit of God," in *Hymns* (Salt Lake City: The Church of Jesus Christ of Latter-day Saints, 1985), no. 2.
20. Jana Riess, *The Next Mormons: How Millennials Are Changing the LDS Church* (New York: Oxford University Press, 2019), 21; emphasis added.
21. Bednar, in "Panel Discussion."

22. All participant names are pseudonyms to preserve anonymity.
23. Neal A. Maxwell, "Apply the Atoning Blood of Christ," *Ensign*, November 1997, 22.
24. Name used with permission.
25. Nelson, "Come, Follow Me," 90.
26. Name used with permission.
27. We are indebted to Justin Hendricks for these three insights.

CHAPTER THREE

Connecting with Heaven through Individual Study and Worship

In this chapter we share two prophetic teachings related to individual study and worship and then share insights about how the *Come, Follow Me* approach has worked for the five hundred Latter-day Saints we surveyed.

Each President of the Church of Jesus Christ is sustained as a prophet, seer, and revelator and, as part of his divine calling, receives prophetic inspiration and revelation from the Lord about what the Lord wants to teach His people at that time. Thus each prophet has a vision for his time to guide the Lord's covenant people through the particular challenges they face. Less than a year after her husband's call as the seventeenth prophet of this dispensation, Sister Wendy Watson Nelson said of President Russell M. Nelson, "It is as though he's been unleashed. He's free to finally do what he came to earth to do. . . . I've seen him become younger. . . . He was foreordained to be the prophet of God on the earth today. He is only reporting to the Lord, and he is fearless with that focus."[1]

President Nelson's focused messages have featured, among others, two recurring teachings: (1) the adversary is real, powerful, and cunning; (2) but even so, soul-saving revelation can come through personal study and worship. We now briefly discuss the dark reality of teaching 1 and the hope-filled message of teaching 2.

TEACHING 1: THE ADVERSARY IS REAL, POWERFUL, AND CUNNING

While Christian denominations are founded on Christ and invite their members to follow Him, some have almost abandoned serious consideration of the devil, the destroyer, or the adversary, as Satan is referred to in the scriptures, regarding him as something of a mythical character unworthy of serious notice or discussion. Conversely, in the Book of Mormon, the ancient prophet Nephi presents a vivid picture of a very real and dynamic being who "rages":

> The devil will grasp them with his everlasting chains, and they be stirred up to anger, and perish;
>
> For behold, at that day shall he rage in the hearts of the children of men, and stir them up to anger against that which is good. (2 Nephi 28:19–20)

Nephi further prophesied of a day when many would figuratively lock the devil away in the closet of childish imagination. In that day, the devil would be denied or ignored at personal peril.

> And others will [the devil] pacify, and lull them away into carnal security, . . . and thus the devil cheateth their souls, and leadeth them away carefully down to hell.
>
> And behold, others he flattereth away, and telleth them there is no hell; and he saith unto them: I am no devil, for there is none—and thus he whispereth in their ears, until he grasps them with his awful chains, from whence there is no deliverance. (2 Nephi 28:21–22)

Some, even within the restored Church, bristle at such pointed references to evil and roll their eyes when the prophet invokes and even emphasizes the reality of Satan. Many are more comfortable sharing Walt Kelly's view that "we have met the enemy and he is us."[2] For some, the idea of an actual war against an actual being is a bit too much.

The restored gospel, however, from the First Vision to the present, is replete with warnings of an "enemy" who is an "actual being from the unseen world" (Joseph Smith—History 1:16). Further, perhaps no prophet since the time of Brigham Young has more explicitly drawn attention to this doctrine than President Nelson. A few of many possible recent references from him include the following:

> "My dear brothers and sisters, the assaults of the adversary are increasing exponentially, in intensity and in variety. Our need to be in the temple on a regular basis has never been greater."[3]
>
> "The forces of evil have never raged more forcefully than they do today. As servants of the Lord, we cannot be asleep while this battle rages."[4]
>
> "We all need . . . protection from the cunning wiles of the adversary."[5]
>
> "The adversary is clever. For millennia he has been making good look evil and evil look good [Isaiah 5:20; 2 Nephi 15:20]. His messages tend to be loud, bold, and boastful. . . . [When we live] in a marketing-saturated world constantly infiltrated by noisy, nefarious efforts of the adversary, where *can* we go to hear [our Heavenly Father]?"[6]

In the April 2019 priesthood session of general conference, President Nelson said,

> Brethren, we need to *do* better and *be* better because we are in a battle. The battle with sin is real. The adversary is quadrupling his efforts to disrupt testimonies and impede the work of the Lord. He is arming his minions with potent weapons to keep us from partaking of the joy and love of the Lord.[7]

When the prophet reports a quadrupling of the enemy's efforts, we do not hear an overstatement. We hear a loving and inspired leader who is doing all he can to prevent further losses. In the words of President Dallin H. Oaks,

> My brethren, and my sisters . . . , I hope you know why your leaders give the teachings and counsel we give. We love you, and our Heavenly Father and His Son, Jesus Christ, love you. Their plan for us is the "great plan of happiness" (Alma 42:8). That plan and Their commandments and ordinances and covenants lead us to the greatest happiness and joy in this life and in the life to come. As servants of the Father and the Son, we teach and counsel as They have directed us by the Holy Ghost. We have no desire other than to speak what is true and to encourage you to do what They have outlined as the pathway to eternal life, "the greatest of all the gifts of God" (Doctrine and Covenants 14:7).[8]

Indeed, we live in a challenging time when the adversary rages, but we are not left alone. Our intent is not to incite fear; it is to highlight the counter-question recently posed by a bishop to his ward: "The adversary is quadrupling his efforts. Are we quadrupling *our* efforts?" Are we shaking off the lethargy and bringing our best? Desperation is not needed, but diligence is. A healthy awareness of the danger that darkness brings can motivate us to seek, invite, and welcome the power that overcomes that destructive danger—the Light of the World.

Increasingly, our current Church leaders have emphasized that we must dig deeper, study more rigorously, experience God more deeply, and connect with Him on an individual level. Specifically, our individual worship needs to include intentional, continual improvement or repentance. President Nelson further explained that we are in the midst of a battle where "if we are to have any hope . . . , we must learn to receive revelation."[9] This phrase leads us to another of President Nelson's oft-repeated teachings that inspires and offers specific hope.

TEACHING 2: SOUL-SAVING REVELATION CAN COME THROUGH PERSONAL WORSHIP

A central question of this book is "How do we help our rising generations go 'all in' rather than opt out?" President Nelson said, "I give you my assurance that regardless of the world's condition and your personal circumstances, you can face the future with optimism and joy if you have faith in the Lord Jesus Christ and His gospel."[10]

A revelatory and continually repentant walk toward the light is not an easy one, but the Light of the World promises, "Draw near unto me and I will draw near unto you" (Doctrine and Covenants 88:63). Remember that according to Elder Neil L. Andersen, "repentance is not the backup plan; it is the plan."[11] If we exercise the faith, courage, and humility to continue that walk toward the light that is the tree of life (continually repenting along the way), the promise is that there will come a day when we will "know even [as we are] known" (1 Corinthians 13:12), a day when all that our Father has will be ours. How do we reach that day?

In response to that question, let us consider the basic, so-called Primary answers of "read and pray" for a moment. In our efforts to live out the Primary answers of "read and pray," recent data show that we as a people have room for improvement. Jana Riess reports:

> In Mormonism, prayer and scripture study often go hand in hand; church members are taught to do both daily. However, the [recent "Next Mormons Survey"] showed that across all generations, daily scripture study was not quite as common as daily prayer. Only 38 percent of all [Church members] read the scriptures every day, and there's little variation by generation.[12]

Even if we improve, however, the "read and pray" response may not be enough. Latter-day Saint historian Patrick Mason has observed that

> [the] Sunday School answers we gave as teenagers aren't always sufficient for adult questions and problems. . . . Grown-up questions require grown-up answers. The Primary answers—read, pray, go to church, be good—never cease to be important, even foundational. But

life becomes more complicated and morally complex as we grow up, so it is essential for our religion to mature with us.[13]

Will merely reading and praying do this difficult "grown-up" work? A couple of quick scripture verses and a perfunctory prayer will probably not yield the needed strength. Sister Becky Craven, Second Counselor in the Young Women General Presidency, stated, "There is a careful way and a casual way to do everything, including living the gospel."[14] Brigham Young taught, "The men and women who desire to obtain seats in the celestial kingdom will find that they must battle everyday [sic]."[15] In the words of Elder Cook, "World conditions increasingly require deepening individual conversion to and strengthening faith in Heavenly Father and Jesus Christ and His Atonement."[16]

How prophetic the words of Elder Neal A. Maxwell now seem, as delivered to BYU students in 1978 in an address since titled "A More Determined Discipleship":

> Make no mistake about it, brothers and sisters, in the months and years ahead, events are likely to require each member to decide whether or not he will follow the First Presidency. Members will find it more difficult to halt longer between two opinions. . . .
>
> . . . In short, brothers and sisters, not being ashamed of the gospel of Jesus Christ includes not being ashamed of the prophets of Jesus Christ! . . .
>
> . . . Concern over the institution of the family will be viewed as untrendy and unenlightened. . . .
>
> It may well be that . . . our time comes to "suffer shame for his name" (Acts 5:41). . . . Remember, as Nephi and Jacob said, we must learn to endure "the crosses of the world" and yet to despise "the shame of it" (2 Nephi 9:18; Jacob 1:8). To go on clinging to the iron rod in spite of the mockery and scorn that flow at us from the multitudes in that great and spacious building seen by Father Lehi, which is the "pride of the world" (1 Nephi 11:36)—is to disregard the shame of the world.[17]

Elder Maxwell's foreshadowed "years ahead," when the Saints would find it difficult to halt between two opinions, seem to have arrived. Will we be strong enough to ignore the pointing fingers of scorn and press forward, clinging to the iron rod? The needed strength can come, in part, from the individual study and worship invitations in *Come, Follow Me*. However, the aim of the prophets with both *Come, Follow Me* and the focus on home-centered worship is not merely to invite us to "read and pray." The identified purpose and blessing presented by Elder Cook are "deepening conversion to Heavenly Father and the Lord Jesus Christ and strengthening faith in Them."[18] Our leaders have continually invited and urged us not to merely read and pray but to learn and worship with all our heart, might, mind, and strength. Indeed, Elder Maxwell taught that scholarship, whether sacred or secular, is a form of worship when done with a heart of consecration.[19]

Elder Maxwell and President Eyring have both pleaded with the Saints not to throw away the foundational Primary answers but to apply them in a grown-up way. They do not dismiss the "read, pray, go to church, be good" mantra that has been identified as foundational but insufficient. Instead, our prophetic leaders urge us to nurture a maturing progression in which (1) "reading" scriptures grows into profound study and pondering of the "best books"; (2) "praying" moves from rattling off a wish list to communicating and communing with God; (3) "going to church" becomes elevated to building Zion through ministering (including serving people to whom we are not "assigned"); and (4) "being good" is not merely sitting quietly with our arms folded but having the meaning of our capstone covenant of consecration revealed to us and then using our hands to give, to bless, and to live out the charity-based covenant of consecration. Elder Maxwell, like the Prophet Joseph Smith, taught, "The Gospel places heavy stress on the individual and his ultimate challenge to govern himself according to righteous principles."[20]

To restate, President Nelson's focused messages have featured, among others, two recurring teachings: (a) the adversary is real, powerful, and cunning; and (b) seeking personal revelation through study and worship of the Father and our Savior can help us overcome "the enemy of [our] soul" (2 Nephi 4:28).

Next, we share dozens of comments from Latter-day Saints who are striving and often struggling to apply the *Come, Follow Me* approach in their lives.

CONNECTING WITH HEAVEN THROUGH INDIVIDUAL STUDY AND WORSHIP

In the context of helping the Saints combat the influences of the adversary and better study the gospel, our inspired leaders have extended the *Come, Follow Me* invitation and provided several related resources. During the first year of *Come, Follow Me*, two stake presidents gave us the opportunity to construct and administer a survey to members of their stakes about their experience with the *Come, Follow Me* invitation at both the individual and family levels. More than five hundred members from stakes in two US locations that are two thousand miles apart responded to the survey. Many responses reflected challenges and barriers they faced in their efforts to study and worship on both personal and family levels. We are grateful to these members who shared their experiences and ideas so that other members might receive encouragement and inspiration. We hope that as you read what many Church members reported about their personal and family efforts to respond to the *Come, Follow Me* initiative, you will receive inspiration about your own personal, couple, and family approach.

One older sister said, "I do not [know] why, but I [am] not doing it." A young mother said, "[I've] had a hard time implementing it." Another said that she's "not doing any of it." Other comments like "[I'm] still working on this" recurred. So did reports like that of a brother who said, "[I] started off great for the first few months, but it slowly decline[d]," and another brother who said, "[I] need to make it a much higher priority." Some said, "[If you are struggling], you're not alone!" Other expressed challenges included the following:

> "It has been hard because I am a widow and live alone. I have tried to always read the lessons each week and implement what I can, [but] it's been a little hard."

> A father of several young children said, "I feel very overwhelmed by everything I have to do already. It will take me some time to figure out how to properly implement it into my life and schedule."

> "I am single, and my two single sons are not active in the Church, so I study all by myself."

"My husband has not been interested in studying the material together, so I do it on my own. I was hoping things would be different with the new emphasis on home learning, but that has not happened for us as a couple."

"Since I live alone, I cherish the times when I can meet with family or friends to discuss and understand the ideas more deeply."

"As a divorced sister without family . . . it is even more isolating."

"I study on my own. My husband and I do not study well together."

"I'm a single dad, so time is always a challenge, whether it's time to cook the dinner or study scriptures. There rarely is enough time."

"It's been really hard for me, because my kids keep me busy all day, every day, [and] my husband is not a member. I can't seem to find the time to study."

The challenges faced and reported by members were many. Indeed, the gap between our ideals and what we actually do can be a source of divine discontent for all of us, but some pragmatic tips can be helpful in narrowing the gap between where we are and where we hope to be. Elder Neal A. Maxwell defined "divine discontent" as the result that comes when we compare "what we are [to] what we have the power to become."[21] Sister Michelle D. Craig, First Counselor in the Young Women General Presidency, said:

> Each of us, if we are honest, feels a gap between where and who we are, and where and who we want to [be and] become. We yearn for greater personal capacity. We have these feelings because we are daughters and sons of God, born with the Light of Christ yet living in a fallen world. These feelings are God given and create an urgency to act.[22]

SOME IDEAS FOR INDIVIDUAL-LEVEL STUDY AND WORSHIP

We now relay some ideas that reportedly benefited some of the surveyed members in their individual-level *Come, Follow Me* study and worship. Some members focused on physical and structural aids they found helpful:

> "I have made a study notebook with everything the lesson references in one place, including the new supplemental materials that became available last month."

> "[I] use the Church website to help [me] with [my] studies."

> "The Book of Mormon videos are wonderful!"

Other members focused on advice related to helpful techniques, approaches, or processes:

> "[I] strive to concentrate on the 'thought questions.'"

> "We read the chapters as individuals in our family, and then three days a week, we do the family activities in the manual."

> "Experiment, and be open to trying new things—talk to friends, get ideas, adjust it to fit your situation, and try, try, try until you find something that works for you."

> "Learn to study, spend time in the scriptures. . . . Go to the Lord in prayer for guidance and for further light and knowledge. Revel in the joy that comes from learning by the Spirit."

> "Listen carefully to the Spirit as you study. The Holy Ghost will whisper your own special lessons to you."

Other members talked about spiritual and personal issues, including patience and endurance:

> "Don't run faster than you have strength. Do what you can, and let the Atonement cover the rest."

"Just keep striving to do it, and eventually it will get easier and blessings will come."

"Be patient with yourself. God wants you to improve, but everyone does so at different rates. The message I got from General Authorities is to do what works for you. . . . If that means that you don't follow the schedule that everyone else is on exactly, that is totally fine. Giving up on it would be a failure, but God just wants us to keep trying to make this a part of our lives."

We are grateful for the feedback and insights from these Church members who, like all committed Saints in all times and places, are pressing forward with a mixture of failures and successes.

The most frequently recurring advice involved the habit of setting a select time each day. Examples of this included the following:

"I have tried to study each day at a specific time."

"I do a spiritual thought with my children each morning that is usually [based on] whatever stood out to me in yesterday's independent reading."

"I study every morning before anything else. I have started getting up earlier so I can get more time. It hasn't been as hard as I anticipated to get up. The time flies!"

"Set a routine/schedule that works best for you, and allow enough time to 'feast' upon the word."

To facilitate a daily rhythm and consistency in their gospel study, some people set a daily reminder on their phone. Others have more concrete reminders like a "prayer rock" beside the bed, while one husband reportedly placed his scriptures over the top of the remote control to give a friendly self-reminder regarding what mattered first and most.

We now briefly turn to two related and insightful statements from Ralph Waldo Emerson regarding human behavior. The first was a favorite of President Heber J. Grant[23] and reads, "That which we persist in doing becomes easier to do, not that the nature of the thing has changed but that our power to do has increased."[24] The hardest steps are the first steps, but the journey is worth taking. To Emerson is also attributed the gem "Sow a thought and you reap an action; sow an act and you reap a habit; sow a habit and you reap a character; sow a character and you reap a destiny."[25] This insight served as a portion of the inspiration for President Monson's teaching that "decisions determine destiny."[26] It seems that the conviction and effort to actively form the habit of daily gospel learning and worship are one of those decisions that can help elevate our eternal destiny.

In addition to the selected responses from members who shared their reflections, we have also benefited from inspired insights from BYU students in our classes. The following from one of our students who wrote about a Sunday practice in her family is shared with her permission:

> **Power Hour.** When I reflect back on the years I spent living at home and how we spent our Sundays, I can distinctly remember "power hour." Power hour was held at a designated time every single Sunday. This hour was for each member of my family to individually do something that helps increase your spirituality and helps you feel/grow closer to the Lord. This could be Personal Progress, indexing, Faith in God, studying scriptures, family history work, journaling, . . . etc. This looked different to everyone, because it was a personal and prayerful thing for each person. Truly anything that helped you feel the Spirit and feel the reverence of the Sabbath day. All my parents asked of us was one hour.
>
> There were a few things that I loved about power hour. The first is the feeling that came into our whole home. There truly is a power that comes when every member of my 7-person family is quietly spending time learning of our Savior and Father in Heaven simultaneously. Our house would be silent, and there would be no interactions between anyone, but everyone could feel of that power. A power that united our family closer together, a power that brought the Spirit so strongly into our house, a power that removed any contention and invited light, and a power that helped us closely feel of our Savior's love.

Another thing I loved about power hour is how my parents were fully involved in it as well as the children. It wasn't a "Go do it, kids, so you leave us alone for an hour after church to take a nap." It was a full family event, and every single person was involved. This experience would not have had the same powerful effect if my parents didn't participate with all of us.

Sacrifice is an important part of our church, and power hour was a great way to incorporate this principle in our lives. No phones, no games, no naps, just one simple hour dedicated to the Lord. This principle instilled a love for the Sabbath day inside of me as a young kid, because I saw what careful observance of this day did for my family. We were strengthened and happier and better because of it.

We find this kind of family-supported but agency-honoring approach to fostering personal study and worship instructive and inspiring. Note that it is simultaneously firm and flexible.

FLEXIBILITY, ADAPTABILITY, CREATIVITY, AND STABILITY

In the area of home-centered religious practice, tradition and structures are good but so are fresh life and creativity. In this process of establishing and maintaining an approach to home-centered gospel living, it will be important for members to balance stability and creativity. It will be important to find ways to initiate processes that are simple, doable, practical, and sustainable. It will also be important to find ways to creatively combine the preferences of different spouses and children into processes that are enjoyable for people with different temperaments, personalities, ages, and degrees of commitment to the gospel and to home-centered religious practices.

On a personal note from us as authors, we are both spouses in what may be called "Latter-day Saint hybrid marriages"—meaning a marriage between a "lifer" (someone raised in the Church) and a convert (someone who joined the Church as an adult). We have experienced the benefits of combining the heritage, tradition, and gospel stability that a "lifer" can bring with the excitement, zeal, sincerity, and gratitude for the gospel that a convert can offer. Perhaps this is one expression of the "grafting" of "young and tender branches" into the tame but old (and even decaying) olive tree.

This fresh grafting gives renewed life to the vineyard to "bring forth again the natural fruit, which natural fruit is good and the most precious above all other fruit" (Jacob 5:8, 61).

Warning against rigidity and overregimentation, Elder Cook specifically emphasized flexibility and adaptability in members' efforts to implement *Come, Follow Me*. The encouragement from the Lord's living Apostles has been to seek revelation and to find what works best in our individual and family situations. On the note of doing what works best personally, we were struck by the following responses to our questions about implementing *Come, Follow Me* that we received almost back to back from two different people:

> **Sister A:** I especially enjoy using technology in my studying.
>
> **Sister B:** Learn to study, spend time in the scriptures, get away from your electronic devices.

Elder Cook might urge each sister to carry on with whatever works best for her. Finding out what works best for you will likely take time, error, and adjustment. We appreciated the following counsel from a parent:

> Allow yourself to do poorly. It's better to try poorly and then slowly improve than to never begin at all or to allow yourself to feel overwhelmed to the point of simply avoiding making the necessary changes. Don't be embarrassed by your failures. Use them as a jumping-off point.

We also appreciated that several Saints who shared their reflections on *Come, Follow Me* focused on the possibility of us learning from others while avoiding comparing ourselves with them. In a BYU devotional titled "Wrestling with Comparisons," Professor J. B. Haws said, "Our perfect, loving God makes no horizontal comparisons."[27] If horizontal comparison is not a divine activity, we should probably avoid it ourselves. However, if we can restrain ourselves from horizontal comparison while still learning vicariously from others' successes, we can be blessed by others' insights.

THE RECENT EXPERIENCES OF MEMBERS

We focus here on members' experiences involving their individual-level study and worship with *Come, Follow Me*.

> A young woman said, "It's more in depth, it's more studying than just plain reading."

> A single woman said, "I'm learning to understand and love the scriptures more deeply. I feel motivated to . . . study the scriptures; I love feeling the Spirit urge me to do so."

> An older mother with children no longer at home said, "I live alone, so I don't study with family, but even by myself, I find I am going more in depth in every way."

> Another single woman said she has also enjoyed "the depth" of her study and "being able to study at [her] own pace and level, relying on doctrine, Church history, scholarship and the Spirit."

Such responses echo Elder Neal A. Maxwell's words:

> The need for greater individual study of the gospel—more scholarship on the part of individual members who do not demand of the Church that it supply them with intellectual handouts—is . . . something which can start to be met in the home. We can be much more effective as leaders and followers if we engage in individual gospel scholarship.[28]

Other experiences with *Come, Follow Me* shared by diverse Saints included the following:

> A young mother said, "I love how much I'm learning. I've honestly never read the Bible through, and I've discovered so much about Jesus Christ's life."

> An older sister said, "I'm learning to understand and love the scriptures more deeply."

Another member said, "It has helped grow my testimony."

An older empty-nest father said, "I am grateful to meet with my fellow members of the Church who are . . . bring[ing] the scriptures alive in their own lives."

To conclude this chapter, we turn to a family from our American Families of Faith Project to illustrate an encouraging pattern—not for purposes of comparison but for purposes of inspiration.

THE PETERSONS: INDIVIDUAL WORSHIP IN AN EXEMPLARY FAMILY

Perhaps no family we have interviewed better illustrated the power of individual study and worship than Jessica and Joseph Peterson,[29] a nondenominational Christian family from Pennsylvania that we interviewed for several hours. Joseph said of Jessica, "I see her get up every morning and take time to read scripture and pray, and I just see that it's not separate from the rest of her day and that it influences the way she does [everything]—the way she interacts with me and the kids and everybody in the community. It's central, it's pervasive."

Jessica later reflected on the depth of her reading and praying in a way that was devotional, personal, and relational. Notably, she did not discuss reading and prayer as "activities." She referred to her study as her "personal time . . . spent with the Lord":

> I think that time spent with the Lord is essential. Personal time. We meet every week in meetings . . . and learn scripture and things, but I think it all comes down to our personal relationship with [God], and that has to come on an individual basis. Just like any other friendship, if you want to get [to] know someone, you need to spend time [with them]. You need to focus on them and listen to them and talk to them and let them into your heart. It's the same thing with God. We could go to church every day of the week, but if we didn't make time when we just got face to face with God alone, I don't think our relationship with Him would grow.

In our exploration of families and faith, we have repeatedly observed what we call "the principle of lived invitation." Specifically, this principle posits, "*Our behavior is permission to others to behave similarly . . . but it is more than that. It is an invitation to do so.*"[30]

Jessica's example, or lived invitation, had a profound impact on Joseph, who chose over the years to follow a similar pattern of making "face-to-face" time with the Lord. Joseph's decision to engage in focused, personal study and prayer gradually changed him. Jessica said of Joseph, "In our family . . . [Joseph's] an excellent role model. The kids need to be able to look up to him and see God in his life . . . [so] that they'll want to pattern their lives after him. It's always great for kids to be able to look up to their dad and see someone that they respect."

In Jessica's earlier discussion of her time spent with the Lord, we see a relationship. In Joseph, we see the worship-based principle of repentance and divinely inspired change. Indeed, it took considerable time for Joseph to become the man that he now is. Jessica said:

> I've seen him changing over the years. He loves the Lord and wants to do what pleases Him . . . modeling what he sees as being valuable for the kids to see. He has an important role in being like Jesus to the kids. A lot of our understanding of who God is comes through fathers, because God is presented as a father in the Bible. If a kid grows up having a father who is loving and kind and supportive and strong, I think it is easier for them to understand God and who He is. . . . The kids see in their father aspects of God, a perfect God.

Joseph saw a godly example in his wife's life and now strives to serve as a similar model for their children. Joseph's next comment deflected Jessica's praise, but like Jessica, he focused on his relationship with God:

> I fall way short and still have a lot that . . . I mess up on, but . . . [when you're] a dad . . . you see your kids make efforts to please you and to do what you want and to imitate you, [and] you don't get upset that they didn't do better. It's just amazing that they even want to try, you know?

So rather than focus on the shortcomings, it's just about trying to relate to God and to get to know Him better.

Later in her interview, Jessica again spoke of her foundational relationship with God and explained, "When you get to that point, when you realize that He cares about you as a person and that He's real, someone who's here even though we can't see Him, [then you grasp] the reality of Him loving us beyond what we can now understand. That is the beginning [of a different kind of life]."

For Jessica and Joseph, what does that different kind of life look like? They now devote a significant portion of their time, energy, and money to constructing wells and schools in a developing area in Africa. Their years of devoted individual study and worship through "face-to-face time with the Lord" have culminated in the consecration of their time, talents, and resources. They have indeed answered Jesus's call to "follow [Him]" (Luke 18:22), and they inspire us to do likewise.

So, what can we learn about individual worship from Jessica and Joseph?

1. You start where you are. For Joseph, that meant making significant changes.
2. One person's loving example, or "lived invitation"—in their case, Jessica's—may spread to others in the family.
3. There is no substitute for alone, "face-to-face" time with God (personal study, worship, and communing are vital).

In connection with the third point, we turn to the words of Joseph Smith:

> The things of God are of deep import, and time and experience, and careful and ponderous and solemn thoughts can only find them out, thy mind O Man, if thou wilt lead a soul into Salvation must stretch as High as the utmost Heavens, and search into and contemplate the darkest abyss, and expanse of eternity. Thou must commune with God.[31]

CONCLUSION

The ideas and suggestions in the *Come, Follow Me* manual are an invitation to study, to learn, to connect and commune with God—and to walk the covenant path to eternal life. President Nelson said, "Commandments are given to liberate one from the bondage of sin and error. The way to joy is to keep the commandments of God. . . . Stay on the covenant path. And if you've stepped off, find your way back."[32]

In a later address, President Nelson said, "I leave my love and blessing upon you, that you may feast upon the word of the Lord and apply His teachings in your personal lives."[33] He has also taught that salvation is an individual matter, one tied to individual study and worship. Exaltation, however, is a family matter. We turn to the matter of family study and worship in the next chapter.

QUESTIONS TO ENCOURAGE CONTEMPLATION AND CONVERSATION

1. President Nelson has reminded us that the adversary is real, powerful, and cunning and that he is "quadrupling his efforts." What evidence have you seen of this during your life?

2. President Nelson has taught that the adversary has millennia of experience in "making good look evil and evil look good" and that his "messages tend to be loud, bold, and boastful." Have you seen evidence of this during your life?

3. President Nelson has taught that, in contrast to the adversary, "messages from our Heavenly Father are strikingly different" and that "He communicates simply [and] quietly." What are the implications of this contrast?

4. How can we build upon the foundational basics of "read, pray, and be good" so that our faith matures from a Primary level to fuller maturity without us becoming intellectually prideful?

5. What are some of the largest barriers you have faced in your individual learning and worship? What pragmatic tips shared by others in this chapter would be helpful? How could you apply them to your own circumstances?

6. Consider the two prophet-endorsed phrases (attributed to Emerson) that were considered in this chapter. How might these insights relate to individual study and worship?

7. The principle of lived invitation states, "Our behavior is permission to others to behave similarly . . . but it is more than that. It is an invitation to do so." How does this principle apply to *Come, Follow Me*? How does this principle apply in other areas of life?

8. Joseph Peterson eventually followed the example of his wife, Jessica, and engaged in his own personal study and worship. What principles are taught by Jessica's example, and how can we emulate the best of those principles?
9. Jessica believes that there is no substitute for alone, "face-to-face" time with God, and President Nelson has repeatedly emphasized the importance of personal revelation. How do these ideas relate to your life?

CREATING OPPORTUNITIES FOR REVELATORY EXPERIENCES (CORE)

1. What intentions do you have to enjoy personal revelatory experiences?
2. How can you and your loved ones encourage each other's revelatory experiences?
3. What personal and relational activities might encourage your own revelatory experiences?

NOTES

1. Quoted in "Latter-day Saint Prophet, Wife and Apostle Share Insights of Global Ministry," October 30, 2018, https://newsroom.ChurchofJesusChrist.org/article/latter-day-saint-prophet-wife-apostle-share-insights-global-ministry#churchofjesuschrist.
2. Walt Kelly, "We Have Met the Enemy and He Is Us," *Pogo*, April 22, 1971; see https://en.wikipedia.org/wiki/Pogo_(comic_strip).
3. Russell M. Nelson, "Becoming Exemplary Latter-day Saints," *Ensign*, November 2018, 114.
4. Russell M. Nelson, "We Can Do Better and Be Better," *Ensign*, May 2019, 69.
5. Russell M. Nelson, "Ministering," *Ensign*, May 2018, 100.
6. Russell M. Nelson, "Hear Him," *Ensign*, May 2020, 89.
7. Nelson, "We Can Do Better," 67–68.
8. Dallin H. Oaks, "Where Will This Lead?," *Ensign*, May 2019, 62.
9. Russell M. Nelson, "Revelation for the Church, Revelation for Our Lives," *Ensign*, May 2018, 96.
10. Russell M. Nelson, "Look Forward to the Future with Faith," *New Era*, June 2018, 5.
11. Quoted in Sarah Jane Weaver, "Repentance Is Not a Backup Plan; It Is the Plan, Says Elder Andersen," *Church News*, July 3, 2018, https://www.ChurchofJesusChrist.org/church/news/repentance-is-not-a-backup-plan-it-is-the-plan-says-elder-andersen.
12. Jana Riess, *The Next Mormons: How Millennials Are Changing the LDS Church* (New York: Oxford University Press, 2019), 151.
13. Patrick Q. Mason, *Planted: Belief and Belonging in an Age of Doubt* (Salt Lake City: Deseret Book, 2015), 80.
14. Becky Craven, "Careful versus Casual," *Ensign*, May 2019, 10.
15. *Discourses of Brigham Young*, sel. John A. Widtsoe (Salt Lake City: Deseret Book, 1954), 392.
16. Quentin L. Cook, "Deep and Lasting Conversion to Heavenly Father and the Lord Jesus Christ," *Ensign*, November 2018, 10.
17. Neal A. Maxwell, "A More Determined Discipleship," *Ensign*, February 1979, 69–70.

18. Cook, "Deep and Lasting Conversion," 9.
19. See Neal A. Maxwell, "The Disciple-Scholar," in Henry B. Eyring, ed., *On Becoming a Disciple-Scholar* (Salt Lake City: Bookcraft, 1995), 7.
20. Quoted in *The Neal A. Maxwell Quote Book*, ed. Cory H. Maxwell (Salt Lake City: Bookcraft, 1997), 170.
21. Neal A. Maxwell, "Becoming a Disciple," *Ensign*, June 1996, 16.
22. Michelle D. Craig, "Divine Discontent," *Ensign*, November 2018, 53.
23. Heber J. Grant often quoted this statement. An excerpt from *Teachings of Heber J. Grant* reads, "Throughout his life, Heber J. Grant worked diligently to improve himself, believing that 'every individual can improve from day to day, from year to year, and have greater capacity to do things as the years come and the years go.' He became known for his persistence, and it was said of him that 'he never criticized other men's weaknesses but made war on his own.'" *Teachings of Heber J. Grant* (Salt Lake City: The Church of Jesus Christ of Latter-day Saints, 2002), 33.
24. Ralph Waldo Emerson, "Quotes," Goodreads, https://www.goodreads.com/quotes/19755-that-which-we-persist-in-doing-becomes-easier-to-do.
25. Ralph Waldo Emerson, "Quotes," Goodreads, https://www.goodreads.com/quotes/416934-sow-a-thought-and-you-reap-an-action-sow-an.
26. Thomas S. Monson, "Decisions Determine Destiny" (Brigham Young University devotional, November 6, 2005), 3, speeches.byu.edu.
27. J. B. Haws, "Wrestling with Comparisons" (Brigham Young University devotional, May 7, 2019), 2, speeches.byu.edu.
28. Quoted in *The Neal A. Maxwell Quote Book*, ed. Cory H. Maxwell (Salt Lake City: Bookcraft, 1997), 144.
29. As mentioned previously, participants' names used in this book are pseudonyms to protect identity and anonymity, as required in research.
30. Loren D. Marks and David C. Dollahite, *Religion and Families: An Introduction* (New York: Routledge, 2016), 14; emphasis in original.
31. Joseph Smith, "History, 1838–1856, volume C-1 [2 November 1838–31 July 1842]," The Joseph Smith Papers, p. 904[b], https://www.josephsmithpapers.org/paper-summary/history-1838-1856-volume-c-1-2-november-1838-31-july-1842/86.
32. Quoted in Jason Swensen, "New First Presidency Answers Questions about Church's Challenges and Opportunities," *Church News*, January 16, 2018, https://www.ChurchofJesusChrist.org/church/news/new-first-presidency-answers-questions-about-churchs-challenges-and-opportunities.
33. Nelson, "Becoming Exemplary Latter-day Saints," 114.

CHAPTER FOUR

Strengthening Faith and Conversion through Family Gospel Study

As we discussed in the last chapter, personal study and worship provide pathways to joyful gospel living because when we worship God individually, we can receive revelatory experiences that provide "soul-to-soul" communication and conversion. The First Vision stands as a historic example that studying and pondering the scriptures and offering sincere prayers can open the heavens and yield personal revelatory experiences ("If any of you lack wisdom, let him ask of God" [James 1:5]). Personal worship of our Heavenly Father, in and of itself, is a marvelous and essential part of our love and devotion to God and serves as a pathway to the prophetic purposes of "strengthening faith" and "deepening conversion."[1] In many cases, faith and conversion come first in one's own life, and then they can be shared in the lives of others. In other cases, shared revelatory experiences take place when members of a couple, a family, a class, a congregation, or the whole Church unitedly experience an outpouring of the Holy Spirit.

Jesus told Peter, "I have prayed for thee, that thy faith fail not; and when thou art converted, strengthen thy brethren" (Luke 22:32). In this single verse, we see a divinely endorsed pattern of conversion: (1) Jesus is fully converted; (2) His personal worship and prayer include praying to His Father for Peter's conversion; (3) in the eternal cycle of true faith, Jesus's vision is that a converted Peter will "strengthen [his] brethren" (individually and together); and (4) those converted brethren will then take the gospel to others ("Go ye therefore, and teach all nations" [Matthew 28:19]).

As we discussed extensively in chapters 1 and 2, this divine pattern was established in the very beginning in the premortal council and then with our first parents, Adam and Eve (see Moses 5:1–12; 6:55–62). It also was discussed and modeled repeatedly in the Book of Mormon (see 2 Nephi 25:23–26) and reiterated by the Lord in this dispensation (see Doctrine and Covenants 68:25; 93:40). We note that the Book of Mormon stresses the importance of parents writing about their own conversion and other sacred experiences. The clearest example of this is Nephi stating that "we labor diligently to write, to persuade our children, and also our brethren, to believe in Christ" and that "we write . . . that our children may know to what source they may look for a remission of their sins" (2 Nephi 25:23, 26). This divine pattern also is exemplified in Alma the Younger (see Alma 36:17–18). In Alma's case, a son remembered a father teaching him of the Savior, which led him to pray and make miraculous personal changes.

The vision is both simple and profound. We personally connect "vertically" with our Father and our Savior as the sources of light and truth. We then become infused with this light and truth, and then we "horizontally" help to bless others through sharing, living, and teaching the light and truth.[2] Following the example of the Lord's servants in all dispensations, we can write about our sacred experiences in order to help our children know in whom we trust.[3] Per our previous discussion of the principle of lived invitation, our best efforts may stimulate a hunger in others to have their own personal connection to the Father and the Son and then hopefully to reach out and strengthen others.

If a deep relationship with a personal God "who is interested in us and who knows us and loves us and wants us to be in a relationship with Him"[4] is the beginning of a new kind of life, the second step is sharing that loving relationship with one's family. In the example of our friends Jessica and

Joseph Peterson, Jessica's personal devotion to God spread to Joseph and eventually to their children.

We note the observation of leading family therapist and researcher William J. Doherty: "During the first six years of life, the template for later life is set down."[5] This is a rare point of consensus among developmental psychologists—that the clay of our humanity seems to be especially malleable and formative during the early years. The Peterson family leveraged this reality and did their best to instill, model, and practice faith with their children during these years.

As the Peterson children reached the teen years, other youth would join them for scripture study and devotionals in their home. Being a musical family, they also integrated traditional, contemporary, and even self-composed music into their worship—which became a faith-promoting power in the lives of many. Jessica said:

> There's nothing more rewarding than helping someone to . . . grow close to the Lord and change to be more like Him. . . . When you are teaching about the Lord and [about] how you feel about God, that's forever. This life is short . . . but when you teach someone . . . how to have God in their life . . . I can't think of a better way to say it than "It's forever."

For Jessica's husband, Joseph, the progression from ungodly and addictive habits to a place of profound relationship with Christ was a walk of faith. Near the end of his interview, Joseph said,

> I don't know where I'd be without [Jesus]. Well, I do know where I'd be without Him. . . . I'd probably be dead or insane or addicted. . . . I'd be a mess.
>
> If [my relationship with God] wasn't there, I wouldn't know who I was. I would be ungrounded, I wouldn't be me without Christ in me. . . . The whole way I construct my understanding of who I am is based in my relationship to God. Really, without that I don't know who I am. . . . In relation to Him, I'm His child. I've been adopted. I'm His heir, I'm His brother, I'm His friend, I'm His servant, I'm His helper.

Joseph would later shift his discussion from the personal to the familial and explain, "As a family [our] hearts are pointed together toward the same thing, and it's God." From Joseph and Jessica, we learn the following:

1. Unified family worship can be enriched by welcoming and strengthening others.

2. We can creatively integrate family strengths into our family worship—for example, music, serving others, hospitality, or food.

3. Joyful, uplifting, home-centered worship is positive, but "when you [also get to] teach someone . . . how to have God in their life," that is an even more beautiful thing.

Would Jessica and Joseph be comfortable being held up as an ideal model of both personal and family worship? No. But when President Nelson urged us toward Spirit-filled, home-centered worship that would "unleash the power of families"[6] and bring remarkable blessings, we thought of families like the Petersons because they show us that these promised blessings can be a reality.

For many members of The Church of Jesus Christ of Latter-day Saints, Joseph's reference to "hearts pointed together toward . . . God" may call to mind similar directions from Alma to the Church of Christ (circa 147 BC) as they gathered together beside the Waters of Mormon. In the Book of Mormon, we read that Alma "commanded [the Church] that there should be no contention one with another, but that they should look forward with one eye, having one faith and one baptism, having their hearts knit together in unity and in love one towards another" (Mosiah 18:21).

In 3 Nephi 18:21, Jesus Himself provided and emphasized a pathway to these blessings: "Pray in your families unto the Father, always in my name, that your wives and your children may be blessed." Along with our friend and colleague Joe Chelladurai, a Saint from India, we published a social science study examining the reported influence of family prayer among 198 diverse American families of faith. Key findings were as follows:

Theme 1: Family prayer [is] a time of family togetherness and interaction

Participants indicated that family prayer was a time of worship, as well as a time of interaction. As they removed distractions and set aside time to disconnect from the rest of the world, they were able to connect with God and each other.

Theme 2: Family prayer [is] a space for social support

Families in the study identify prayer as a place for them to "go to God" to "draw strength" and "comfort and encourage each other." Prayer can also be a time for families to share and process personal challenges. It is a powerful arena for providing and receiving social support.

Theme 3: Family prayer [is] a means for intergenerational transmission of religion

Family prayer is one way to develop a "sense of ritual" as parents teach their children about religion and faith. As children learn to pray through their parents' example, a flow of religious direction and communication occurs.

Theme 4: Family prayer involves issues and concerns of individuals and the family

Not only is prayer an opportunity to speak to God, it is also a time for families to disclose details of their day. Whether it is addressing a concern or an opportunity to pray in behalf of others, prayer becomes a "time and space" to share feelings and thoughts.

Theme 5: Family prayer helps reduce relational tensions

For participants[,] praying together as a family brought a "balancing" effect to their relationships.

Theme 6: Family prayer provides feelings of connectedness, unity and bonding

The physical and spiritual aspects of family prayer—holding hands and coming together as a family "praying as one"—bring a spiritual connection, unity and bonding.[7]

If family prayer alone can yield benefits and blessings like these, it is encouraging to contemplate what family prayer combined with gospel learning and study might facilitate. Certainly, family worship can provide a pathway to unity, love, and joyful gospel living because, as the Savior taught, "Where two or three are gathered together in my name, there am I in the midst of them" (Matthew 18:20).

SOME NOTES ON PAINFUL REALITY

Some readers may fairly say, "This is all very idealistic. Can we talk about the daily, difficult, and sometimes dark reality that seems to pervade our attempts at family worship?" From our interviews with families of faith and from our own family lives, we are acutely aware of how difficult it can be to establish and maintain regular, meaningful, and joyful family religious activities.

The exemplary families we interviewed (across diverse faiths) were often transparent in discussing their own struggles related to gathering their families for home-based worship. For many of us, such reports are all too familiar. Indeed, an additional finding from our study on family prayer was that "families struggle to pray together when there is disunity."[8] This finding draws attention to the importance of asking for, seeking, and offering forgiveness frequently within families—and also emphasizes patience with each other.

Many years ago, Loren was speaking with one of the benevolent grandfathers of the field of family studies, Wes Burr. Loren said with some exasperation, "I recently told my children that like Martin Luther King Jr., I too have a dream. My dream is that one blessed night, I will call my five children for scripture study and family prayer . . . and they will come! Not a word of whining or complaining from them—and no nagging and wheedling from me. . . . They will all just come."

After a chuckle, Wes said, "Loren, don't forget that the way you gather your family may be as important as the scripture study or prayer itself." This is counsel worth remembering.

The perennial question remains, however: Is it worth the struggle? A short while ago, we wrote about this issue for a broad audience in the *Atlantic* and concluded with the following hope:

Ultimately, what seems to matter most about family home evening is not the specific rituals, but that there are rituals at all—that a family decides to set aside a specific time of the week to gather and have a meaningful experience together. Is there perfection in such a family ritual? Never. Is there some effort, hassle, friction, and chaos? Almost always. But is there sometimes a spark of transcendent magic? In truth, it's rare. But the next family home evening might just be one of those nights.[9]

In the words of our friend and colleague Heather Howell Kelley, a young Latter-day Saint wife and mother, family worship can be beautiful and effective, "not every time, but over time."[10]

Rebecca (a Jewish mother of three) expressed concerns about the hassles of family worship in richer context:

> We do the same rituals for our holidays and all our Sabbath activities, and, you know, a lot of times we have to nag the kids and pull them into things, but if we *don't* do something or if something is missed or if we say, "We are not going to do Shabbat," they say [with animation], "What do you mean we're not doing it!?" . . . They'll get mad that we don't do it. They're upset because life is not the way it usually is. They get upset if we don't hallow [the Sabbath]. It's very interesting. Sometimes they act like we are annoying them by dragging them through the ritual, but if we don't have it there for them, they get upset by it. . . . The religion provides a lot of strength and comfort and structure.

Patricia, a member of our own faith, told us the following about her family worship:

> When our children were very young, we used to think, "Why are we doing this? This is crazy. They are not listening to a word." And now, as adults, they will come back and say, "Family home evening was so wonderful!" [Laughs.] You don't realize the impact a lot of things have when you are doing them. . . . They used to fight us tooth and toenail

. . . and now the one who fought us the hardest will do anything to be there. It's payday—you just have to hang in there.

William J. Doherty wrote a book called *The Intentional Family* to emphasize the importance of "intentional" (conscious and planned) family rituals and traditions to help families resist challenges that weaken them.[11] In our interviews, we have found that in relational, structural, emotional, and spiritual ways, religious family practices and shared worship seem to offer many families a stronger sense of family belonging, identity, and security in a rapid-paced world that often rides roughshod over our more sensitive needs—including our hunger for meaning and our need for deep connection with both heaven and with one another. The following lists provide a summary of our findings.[12]

What are the elements of family worship or rituals? What do families actually do?

- They set a given weekly time apart as sacred (for example, Sunday afternoon or Monday evening).
- They pray together.
- They eat together (for example, meals, dessert, or treats).
- They sing sacred (but often lively and fun) music together.
- They study sacred texts together.
- They participate in recreational activities, "breathe," and play together.

What elements of family worship or rituals are transferrable to virtually all families?

- A set time.
- A set place.
- A "set" table (that is, eating together).
- A deep, meaningful, shared sacred purpose.
- A focus on relationships and healthy, uplifting family processes.
- Intentionality.

What are some best practices?[13]

- Seeking and promoting unity through buy-in and consensus for the family practice.
- Avoiding a preachy, heavily parent-directed approach to the practice.
- Seeking to engage all family members as contributors and cocreators instead of only as consumers.
- Focusing on authentic dialogue and conversation across generations and family members.
- Seeking the counsel of children and youth about how to best adapt practices across time.
- Maintaining balance between structure/consistency and adaptability/flexibility.
- Inviting other people or families to occasionally join in and share the sacred family practice.
- Helping the family look outside itself by finding other families to voluntarily serve.
- Remembering that the processes involved in gathering the family matter as much as the practice.

What are the frequently mentioned challenges and obstacles to family worship or rituals?

- It takes time—time for the practice, time for preparation, time for organization.
- Relentless effort and energy are required. ("It is hard.")
- There are recurring scheduling conflicts with outside entities (for example, school, work, or activities).
- Despite the family's efforts to seek unity, there is often internal resistance from children.
- When children are young, it is difficult to maintain order and to prevent chaos and meltdowns.
- With teenagers, it is often difficult to prevent apathy and to promote engagement.

How do family processes interrelate and intersect with family worship or rituals?

- Personal and familial identity are strengthened. (Who am I? Who are we?)
- Positive cohesion and unity are promoted. ("It brings us together.")
- Stability is maintained or restored (for example, through problem solving).
- Structure, predictability, and boundaries are established.
- Dialogic communication is enhanced. ("We can talk.")

Why are family worship or rituals reportedly worth it?

- "It helps keep our marriage close and keeps us on the same page."
- "It helps me feel close to my children."
- "It reminds us of what matters."
- "It keeps God at the center."

Along with several other family researchers, we have published reports containing social scientific evidence of a unifying power in family worship and ritual. We stand by these findings and continue to add to them in our current research efforts with bright and capable BYU students and colleagues from various faiths and universities. With all this said, we have been struck by a careful reading of the prophetic words surrounding the call for home-centered worship and the urgency surrounding *Come, Follow Me*. There is a message that exceeds the typical "family strengthening" that accompanies family rituals. Elder David A. Bednar emphasized:

> Our commitment to learn and live according to truth is increasingly important in a world that is "in commotion" [Doctrine and Covenants 45:26] and is ever more confused and wicked. We cannot expect simply to attend Church meetings and participate in programs and thereby receive all of the spiritual edification and protection that will enable us "to withstand in the evil day" [Ephesians 6:13].[14]

As we have discussed throughout this book (see especially chapters 1 and 2), emphasis on worship and learning in the home is not new. Decades ago, President Harold B. Lee taught, "The most important of the Lord's work you will ever do will be within the walls of your own homes,"[15] and Elder Neal A. Maxwell similarly observed that "the home is usually the place where most of our faith is established and increased, for there we witness the examples of righteous parents as we work out our salvation in a setting that requires love, forgiveness, patience, and all the other virtues. . . . [Our homes] should be a prep school for the celestial kingdom."[16]

Returning to Elder Bednar, we note his emphasis that "our homes are the ultimate setting for learning, living, and becoming."[17] We now share with you the insights of some of the more than five hundred Latter-day Saints who shared their early experiences with following the Savior's invitation to "come, follow me" (Luke 18:22) through home-centered family worship.

SOME REAL CHALLENGES

First, we begin with some challenges mentioned by mothers with diverse home situations, all of whom have children at home:

> "[One challenge is] the responsibility of yet another thing I have to do as a wife and mother."

> "It can be difficult to teach to a large age range of children at the same time so all understand."

> "[One challenge is] avoiding the temptation to make it into a 'production.'"

> "[It is a challenge] to use it with very young children and finding time to do it, since I am a single mother."

> "It's been really hard for me, because my kids keep me busy all day, every day, [and] my husband is not a member. I can't seem to find the time to study."

One young mother with four children under the age of eight addressed her *Come, Follow Me* challenges in a talk at a stake conference we attended. She explained that her family does five minutes of study a day. Any more time than that and things get "crazy." She concluded, "It's not an hour, but I think the Lord understands." This young mother's words capture a reality about family gospel study: zero minutes is literally nothing. Conversely, going too long may bring mutiny and chaos. Five minutes a day is a "small thing" that can make a big difference.

Fathers reported their share of challenges as well:

> "The biggest challenge early on was trying to figure out the best way to go through all the material without it being too bloated and long for our young children."

> "I feel very overwhelmed by everything I have to do already."

> "The amount of reading can be quite daunting some weeks. Getting my family to be excited about the program and being willing to actually do it have been hit and miss at best."

> "[It is a real challenge] getting the whole family together for that additional hour of study."

> "[What has been a challenge to me is] accepting the teaching and learnings as my own responsibility."

> "We really can't dwell on gospel matters more than five or ten minutes. The children (teenagers) will lose interest or feel captive if we go too long; they will refuse to participate in the future if they feel overwhelmed by this."

We note the similarity between the last father's quote (five or ten minutes) and the quote from the young mother of four referenced earlier (five minutes). A little time is far better than no time, for as Alma taught, "By small and simple things are great things brought to pass" (Alma 37:6).

Even so, "small things" can involve large challenges. While the above discussions of challenges by mothers and fathers are verbatim, there were many other mentioned challenges that we will visit only briefly and in summary.

FAMILIES' GREATEST CHALLENGES TO HOME-CENTERED GOSPEL LEARNING

Overall, we observed four recurring themes regarding reported challenges to engaging in home-based learning and worship:

1. There is never enough time.
2. There are different levels of involvement and motivation within the family.
3. It is a challenge to get through the material.
4. It is difficult to teach different-aged children and keep everyone engaged.

In addition to home-centered challenges, some parents mentioned challenges related to heavily scheduled Sundays at the ward or branch level. One parent said, "Sometimes a busy Sunday can displace our family discussion."

It is comforting to remember that the "solemn responsibility" and "sacred duty" to rear children in love and righteousness, as taught by prophets in "The Family: A Proclamation to the World," are buttressed by the divinely inspired guidance "In these sacred responsibilities, fathers and mothers are obligated to help one another as equal partners."[18] Equal partnership, or what the scriptures call being "equally yoked" (see 2 Corinthians 6:14), is a divinely inspired doctrine of relational joy, peace, and power. We hope that mothers and fathers, husbands and wives, will work together as equal partners so they can jointly claim prophetically promised blessings. The psychiatrist and Jewish luminary Viktor Frankl said, "If architects want to strengthen a decrepit arch, they increase the load which is laid upon it, for thereby the parts are joined more firmly together. . . . What man actually needs is not a tensionless state but rather the striving and struggling for a worthwhile goal, a freely chosen task."[19]

By joining "firmly together" while under pressure or going through challenges, our marriages and families can bear significant weight without collapsing. Our own research indicates that one key difference between weak or failed marriages and strong, enduring marriages is that in the latter, the husband and wife join "more firmly together" when the responsibilities of life come (including family religious practice) instead of moving away from each other.

Now that we have discussed in this chapter several concerns and challenges that may impede family-level efforts to having home-centered worship, the next chapter presents several reported successes that Latter-day Saints shared in the hope that they would provide encouragement and inspiration for the rest of us.

QUESTIONS TO ENCOURAGE CONTEMPLATION AND CONVERSATION

1. What scriptural examples can you identify of parents teaching their children the plan of happiness and the Savior's central role in the plan?

2. Jesus told Peter, "I have prayed for thee, that thy faith fail not: and when thou art converted, strengthen thy brethren" (Luke 22:32). How does this divine pattern translate to our own personal and family learning and worship?

3. In the Peterson family, we saw that "unified family worship can be enriched by welcoming and strengthening others." Whom might you invite to occasionally (or even consistently) join your family for home-centered gospel study in ways that could bless his or her life? Are there creative, technology-assisted ways you can involve others at a distance?

4. Are there ways that your family can creatively integrate personal or family strengths into your family worship, such as music, hospitality, acting, storytelling, service, or food?

5. We noted several benefits of family prayer. Are there benefits that you have seen in your own family? How can adding family gospel learning to family prayer bless your family members?

6. The latter part of the chapter shares challenges mentioned by both wives and husbands in implementing *Come, Follow Me*. How can we face challenges together in ways that embody the family proclamation's ideal of equal partnership?

CREATING OPPORTUNITIES FOR REVELATORY EXPERIENCES (CORE)

1. What intentions do you have to enjoy personal revelatory experiences?
2. How can you and your loved ones encourage each other's revelatory experiences?
3. What personal and relational activities might encourage your own revelatory experiences?

NOTES

1. Quentin L. Cook, "Deep and Lasting Conversion to Heavenly Father and the Lord Jesus Christ," *Ensign*, November 2018, 9.
2. Enos's prayer and progression of concern in the Book of Mormon reflect a similar pattern (see Enos 1:1–27).
3. See David C. Dollahite, *God's Tender Mercies: Sacred Experiences of a Mormon Convert* (Salt Lake City: By Common Consent Press, 2018). The entire book provides many examples of writing about conversion and sacred experiences for the benefit of one's children and includes an appendix sharing ideas for how to write one's sacred experiences for one's posterity.
4. These words from an anonymous Christian mother were quoted in chapter 2.
5. William J. Doherty, *Take Back Your Kids: Confident Parenting in Turbulent Times* (Notre Dame, IN: Sorin Books, 2000), 43.
6. Russell M. Nelson, "Becoming Exemplary Latter-day Saints," *Ensign*, November 2018, 114.
7. Direct excerpts are from Marianne Holman Prescott, "'The Family That Prays Together Stays Together' Is More Than a Saying, BYU Research Finds," *Church News*, July 27, 2018, https://www.thechurchnews.com/living-faith/2018-07-27/new-byu-research-shares-6-reasons-why-your-family-should-pray-together-47683. For the full journal article, see Joe M. Chelladurai, David C. Dollahite, and Loren D. Marks, "'The Family That Prays Together . . .': Relational Processes Associated with Regular Family Prayer," *Journal of Family Psychology* 32, no. 7 (2018): 849–59. For a shorter, reader-friendly version of the findings, see Loren Marks, David C. Dollahite, and Joe Chelladurai, "Family Prayer: A Sacred Time and a Sacred Space—Findings from a National Study," *Meridian*, March 24, 2019, https://ldsmag.com/family-prayer-a-sacred-time-and-a-sacred-space-findings-from-a-national-study/.
8. Prescott, "Family That Prays Together."
9. David C. Dollahite and Loren Marks, "Mormons' Weekly Family Ritual Is an Antidote to Fast-Paced Living," *Atlantic*, March 29, 2018, https://www.theatlantic.com/family/archive/2018/03/mormon-family-home-evening/556658/.
10. Heather Howell Kelley, email message, October 2020.
11. William J. Doherty, *The Intentional Family: Simple Rituals to Strengthen Family Ties* (New York: HarperCollins, 1999).
12. We have repeatedly observed the power of rituals and shared sacred practices in the exemplary families of faith that we have interviewed, and we chose to include an adapted version of our key findings in the following lists. These lists are adapted from Loren D.

Marks and David C. Dollahite, "'Don't Forget Home': The Importance of Sacred Ritual in Families," in *Understanding Religious Rituals*, ed. John P. Hoffman (New York: Routledge, 2012), 186–203.
13. By "best practices," we mean those practices that seemed to work well for the families that we interviewed.
14. David A. Bednar, "Prepared to Obtain Every Needful Thing," *Ensign*, May 2019, 102.
15. Harold B. Lee, *Strengthening the Home* (Salt Lake City: The Church of Jesus Christ of Latter-day Saints, 1973), 7.
16. Quoted in Cory H. Maxwell, ed., *The Neal A. Maxwell Quote Book* (Salt Lake City: Bookcraft, 1997), 159.
17. Bednar, "Prepared to Obtain," 102.
18. "The Family: A Proclamation to the World," ChurchofJesusChrist.org.
19. Viktor E. Frankl, *Man's Search for Meaning* (Boston: Beacon Press, 2006), 105.

CHAPTER FIVE

Ideas and Encouragement regarding Family Study

Later in this book (chapters 7 and 8), we will share members' reports of how they have seen prophetic promises begin to be fulfilled in their personal and familial lives as they have made imperfect but consistent and faith-filled efforts to study and worship. In this chapter, we present some pragmatic ideas and encouragement from members regarding success within the walls of their own homes. Recurring ideas in hundreds of responses to the question "What has worked well?" included the following:

- To be consistent, it is helpful to have a set time for *Come, Follow Me*.
- For many families, Sunday afternoons and Monday home evening are the most common "larger chunks" of study time.
- Many break *Come, Follow Me* into small (five- to fifteen-minute) chunks daily or weekly.

- Many find that taking personal notes is helpful and meaningful.
- There are a variety of effective approaches to *Come, Follow Me*.
- Many singles deeply appreciate the opportunity to join with family and friends.
- When Saints do personal *and* family study, they report great benefits.

We asked the surveyed members, "If you could give one piece of advice to a person or family who is struggling with the new home-centered, Church-supported approach to gospel learning and the *Come, Follow Me* materials, what would it be?" To be context specific, we share offered ideas, advice, and encouragement from sisters and brothers in various life situations, as indicated.

ENCOURAGEMENT FROM SINGLES

When single sisters were asked for a piece of advice (including sisters who were divorced, widowed, or never married), their reports included the following:

> "Experiment, and be open to trying new things—talk to friends, get ideas."

> "Adjust it to fit your situation, and try . . . until you find something that works for you."

> "Set a routine/schedule that works best for you, and allow enough time to 'feast' upon the word. 'Snacks' are great, but they aren't a feast."

> "Just keep striving to do it, and eventually it will get easier, and blessings will come."

The latter comment seems to reflect Emerson's encouraging wisdom from chapter 3: "That which we persist in doing becomes easier to do, not that the nature of the thing has changed but that our power to do has increased."[1]

A few reports from single brothers (including brothers who were divorced, widowed, or never married) included the following:

"Consistency is the goal for me. Doing our study earlier in the day is a goal for me. Having everyone participate is a goal for me. I'm a single dad, so time is always a challenge, whether it's time to cook the dinner or study scriptures. There rarely is enough time. Quality of our studies is sometimes sacrificed in schedule juggling and too much to do on my schedule, or not getting everyone gathered earlier and . . . end[ing] up doing studies right before bed, which can make studying at that hour hard for a variety of reasons. That is again why consistency is [an] overarching goal and the key for me."

"Living the gospel and following the prophet never was an easy task in any generation of the Church, ancient or modern. Luckily, we have a pattern established by Joseph Smith that is a promised solution to anyone who tries it. Step 1: Seek out all the resources God has already given you to be successful. In *Come, Follow Me*, the opening pages are dedicated to helping us get the most out of our experiences. Step 2: Read and follow the advice given in James 1:5: 'If any of y[ou] lack wisdom, let him ask of God, that giveth to all men liberally, and upbraideth not; and it shall be given him.' Step 3: Follow the inspiration that comes, or be okay with a nonanswer. Step 4: Repeat the process over . . . again. Joseph Smith developed his relationship with God over a lifetime, and their bond became sweeter with every prayer."

"My kids may not always have the most spiritual experience from studying together, but they will sometimes, . . . and they will remember that, and they will learn and remember as they grow that studying daily was important to their dad."

ENCOURAGEMENT FROM THOSE WITH SMALL CHILDREN IN THE HOME

Of all the groups of members surveyed, sisters with small children seemed to be the most taxed and stressed. Accordingly, we share more responses in this section than in any other. We do so for two reasons: (1) to allow these sisters to speak to others in their life stage and (2) to help those of us who are striving to love and support young mothers to better understand their context. Advice, counsel, and encouragement from sisters with small children included the following:

> "[If you are struggling], you're not alone!"

> "God is the first priority. When we trust in serving Him first, everything else will align. Now I need to follow my own advice."

> "[I would tell those who are struggling] not to stress too much. I believe Heavenly Father appreciates our efforts to try, even if they fail and we have to start again."

> "Pray for help. This program is most definitely from heaven, and I think the most difficult part is starting. Try lots of different ways of implementing it, and keep [whatever] works best for you."

> "[Take] three weeks to form a habit, and I know you will see a difference in your life, and it will be possible to carry out this program."

> "Just open the manual up and start small. You can look at the pictures, read the introduction of the lesson for the week, and see where that takes you."

> "SIMPLIFY! Our kids range in age from 2 to 11 and only have attention spans for short times. We try to keep it as simple as possible for them to understand. If our older kids have more questions, then we spend more time talking to them and let our younger kids be done."

> "Don't be embarrassed by your failures. Use them as a jumping-off point."

IDEAS AND ENCOURAGEMENT REGARDING FAMILY STUDY

"The best lie Satan ever told us was 'It's not going to be THE best or YOUR best from the beginning, so why try?'"

"Go to the Church website."

"Just do it. It gets easier. Satan knows the kind of power that comes from strong testimonies, and he wants you to fail. The kids will remember more than you realize, and when they need to draw from those reserves, they will have strength and courage."

"[There is a] power [that] comes from understanding and applying the principles taught from parents who are blessed with revelation to know what the[ir children] need."

"[The value of studying as a family] will be immeasurable in a future day. Our families must have this fortification to withstand what is coming, [so] don't give up."

"I don't know [what advice to give], because I am the one struggling with it."

"Learn it for yourself first, then teach it to your family."

"Don't feel pressure to implement this program the same way that your neighbors do. Sit down as a family, and make your own plan that will work for you. Try it out, evaluate, counsel together, and refine your plan over time."

"The purpose of *Come, Follow Me* is to draw closer to our Savior, Jesus Christ. If you get behind, don't stress out, and don't feel guilty. Just ask Heavenly Father for help, study a little bit every day, and I promise you will receive that blessing of drawing closer to Christ."

Counsel and encouragement regarding *Come, Follow Me* from married fathers with small children in their homes included the following:

"Read *Gospel Teaching and Learning*, which is a remarkable resource published by the Church about how to teach effectively. It has been extremely helpful for us and given us many great ideas."

"If finding the time to gather and [read] and study together is the issue, try to have more meaningful discussions during dinner or other times you're around the family."

"Find the schedule/pattern/timing that helps you enjoy it the most. If you dread it, you will find excuses to put it off. If you enjoy the time, you'll continue growing."

"Make sure you set a time, and hold that time sacred. When your family schedule changes, like in the summer, remember to quickly reset a new time that works for the family so you can keep a consistent schedule."

"Do what works best for you."

"Use the [Gospel] Library!"

"Be patient with yourself. God wants you to improve, but everyone does so at different rates. The message I got from General Authorities is to do what works for your family. If that means that you don't follow the schedule that everyone else is on exactly, that is totally fine. Giving up on it would be a failure, but God just wants us to keep trying to make this a part of our lives."

"Pray to know how your family could best use it, and act on ideas so you can eventually find the best application for your situation."

ENCOURAGEMENT FROM THOSE WITH OLDER CHILDREN AT HOME

Parents with teenage or emerging adult children also offered ideas. Of the several groups of members we studied, only sisters with young children at home seemed to have more on their plates and minds than sisters with older children at home. When asked for one piece of advice, some mothers of older children reported the following:

"[I] can't help. I'm the one struggling."

"Use the Church website to help you with your studies."

"Give yourself some time to really get into the studying."

"Ask to join another family for one time to see how they do it, or visit your own family members for their 'home church' time."

"Keep it simple, and [do it] in small bites."

"We've been promised great blessings that will come to our families by implementing the program, so I study by myself in expectation that those blessings will come."

"Just start! Jump in! You will find a pattern that fits your individual family/yourself, and you will begin to see the blessings of increased faith. . . . Your love for the Savior will grow. You will [gain] increased insight into His person, His character."

"If all the material feels overwhelming, take the time to just study a few portions each week. It will bring the Spirit into your home!"

"Rather than being overwhelmed by a sense that you don't know exactly what you should do and how you should do it, enjoy the greater sense of personal freedom to approach your gospel learning in a way that works best for you."

Counsel and encouragement regarding *Come, Follow Me* from fathers with older children in their homes included the following:

"Try your best each week, and don't beat yourself up if you don't accomplish all you wanted to. Keep working at it until it becomes more of a habit and everyone adjusts."

"Assume the Lord understands you'd like to do better; however, you are trying to do the best under your circumstances. To be doing it . . . can really be the achievement."

"Similar to [home evening], just do it, even when there are bumps along the way."

"Remember . . . that the Lord is on your side, that you can succeed, and that He stands ready to help you. He inspired the Brethren to help us move forward in this way, and He'll help us implement it successfully."

"Seek your children's input, and ask them to think of ways they can help."

"Make the effort to have a set time to study together. It won't happen unless it is a scheduled event each Sabbath or during the week."

A REVIEW OF MEMBER ENCOURAGEMENT REGARDING *COME, FOLLOW ME*

Across the variety of women and men we heard from, most members were interested in doing their best to implement the new home-centered, Church-supported approach to gospel learning offered by *Come, Follow Me*. Despite challenges, often significant ones, many members reported trying to positively respond to this invitation in their lives and homes. Many were also willing to offer encouragement and ideas to fellow Saints who might be struggling—and were also eager to learn what others had done.

There is good reason to believe that efforts by ward, branch, and stake leaders to assist in this process will be met with appreciation from most members. However, agency, adaptability, flexibility, customization, and a willingness to seek and follow the Spirit at an individual and a family level are vital for leaders and members to remember.

EXEMPLARS OF HOME-CENTERED WORSHIP: LEE AND NADIA

We now take an in-depth look at portions of an interview involving home-centered worship with a Latter-day Saint family from our American Families of Faith Project. During past years of his own teen rebellion, the father, Lee,[2] was a deeply talented and intelligent boy floundering in a directionless array that social scientists would call antisocial behavior, complete with the full-length trench coat and wild hair. He met Nadia and was fascinated by her—and eventually by her religious beliefs. Several months later, after a one-week personal immersion in the Book of Mormon, Lee decided to be baptized. He later married Nadia, who was a lifelong member, and they have striven to be "all in" with their individual and shared commitment to the gospel.

For their more than twenty-five years of marriage, Lee and Nadia have studied, loved, and lived their faith while raising their children in a culture that is often hostile and counter to the gospel. However, their faith in God's revealed word has involved both belief and action. Nadia explained:

> One of the most important [practices] for me is family prayer and [studying] scripture verses. It's something that we share with our children.... [When] they [were] still pretty young [and] not able to have deep intellectual discussions about our faith, ... we ... deal[t] with them on their intellectual level. We have family prayer together. We take turns. Each member of the family ... takes turns saying our family prayer at meals or in the morning or at night right before we go to bed. And then each night we gather together, and we study from the scriptures.... When the kids don't understand something, they'll stop us. [We'll talk about] the meaning of a certain word, and [we'll ask], "What [are] they ... talking about here?" And it's a wonderful opportunity for us every day to teach them a little bit more, and to find out what they know, and we never cease to be surprised at how much ... they understand. And doing that every day is something that I hope will continue to instill the knowledge of what we believe.

Did their children experience their own deep and lasting conversions? Our initial interview with Lee and Nadia was more than a decade ago. Our follow-up revealed that their oldest son served an honorable mission and married in the temple. Their oldest daughter served faithfully in a young single adult ward for years before recently marrying in the temple as well. Their youngest son is currently serving a mission. Another daughter, however, has left the Church. Lee and Nadia, like many parents, pray for the return of a beloved child whose current walk is not on the covenant path. (Of course, in every family the religious choices of individual children interact with parental intentions and efforts toward gospel learning and living. Therefore, it is important for all of us to avoid judging parents based on the religious choices of children.)

Many years of Nadia's life involved serving as an early-morning seminary teacher in her ward, but it is her opinion that even her best efforts "will not be enough" for most of the young women and young men she has taught, unless they are getting significant foundational gospel teaching at home and through their own personal study. In her interview, Nadia explained her continual urging to both her own children and to the seminary-aged youth: "You have got to learn and decide for yourself if this [is] true. . . . Yes, my parents raised me with the knowledge of the doctrine that I now hold to, but *I* had to make that choice[, and so will you]."

Similarly addressing both the home-based worship and personal choice, Lee said,

> Family prayer or the study of the scriptures or family home evening . . . it always comes back to *this is what we believe*. And yeah, we all have our different interests or different hobbies, and our different personalities, but we have our religion in common, and it's a rock we all can hold on to. It's always gonna be there, it's never changing, it's there to comfort us. And the teachings that we [learn] through the scriptures . . . these are things that I as a parent . . . need to take into my own life, and in turn lead my family . . . by teaching those things, by living those things, [by] being an example. And without it, we would kind of be blown around by any wind of what's bad [out] there.

Lee also emphasized the responsibility he has felt as a father:

> With our religion, one of the things that is taught is that as parents it is our responsibility to teach our children correct principles and righteous principles and that if we don't, we are going to be held accountable as parents. . . . [I] feel a very strong responsibility to live up [to] that. Now, does that mean that if a kid grows up and doesn't follow, is that my fault? No, but it's my job to teach that kid the correct things, and—hopefully, you know, in our religion we believe in agency, that every person has the right to choose for himself the path that they [want]. . . . But it's our job to present the correct and righteous principles so that they will know right from wrong.

Nadia and Lee's efforts are in some ways exemplary. However, no life is without its challenges. Lee works in a maximum-security prison that at times feels to him to be almost saturated with "pure evil." Lee expressed his strong desire that his home sharply contrast with his work setting:

> There is enough bad influence out there in the world. There are plenty of people and media and whatever that can lead our children astray—can lead them to a place that we don't want them to go. And there is enough of that out there that we don't need to have it in here in our home, within the walls of our home. The walls of our home should be a sanctuary.

PROPHETIC COUNSEL FOR CHALLENGING TIMES

President Nelson's address in April 2018, the conference immediately preceding the unveiling of a home-centered, Church-supported approach to worship, revealed an awareness of the multifaceted challenges that families like Lee and Nadia's face. Specifically, President Nelson stated, "I am . . . not naive about the days ahead. We live in a world that is complex and increasingly contentious. The constant availability of social media and a 24-hour news cycle bombard us with relentless messages. If we are to have any hope of sifting through the myriad of voices and the philosophies of men that attack truth, we must learn to receive revelation."

As foreboding as some of this message is, it is not the whole message. Hope and light abound. President Nelson also emphasized that in spite of the difficulties, we need not despair. He emphasized:

> I am optimistic about the future. . . .
>
> Our Savior and Redeemer, Jesus Christ, will perform some of His mightiest works between now and when He comes again. We will see miraculous indications that God the Father and His Son, Jesus Christ, preside over this Church in majesty and glory. But in coming days, it will not be possible to survive spiritually without the guiding, directing, comforting, and constant influence of the Holy Ghost.
>
> My beloved brothers and sisters, I plead with you to increase your spiritual capacity to receive revelation.[3]

The foundational and preparatory work for some of the Savior's "mightiest works" may be laid by families (like Lee and Nadia's) who strive to make their home a sanctuary from the world.

We return to the model illustrated by the Savior to Peter as addressed at the outset of the last chapter. Again, the Lord's words to the man who would become Cephas, "the Rock," were "I have prayed for thee, that thy faith fail not: and when thou art converted, strengthen thy brethren" (Luke 22:32).

Individual and family study and worship are pathways to joyful gospel living because when we worship God personally and together, we can experience a fulness of joy (see 3 Nephi 17:20), as Jesus did when worshipping the Father with ancient American families following His Resurrection. Studying the teachings of Jesus alone or with others is a pathway to joyful gospel living. As the Savior said, "These things have I spoken . . . that your joy might be full" (John 15:11).

In this chapter, we heard ideas and encouragement from a diverse array of members of the Church of Jesus Christ. We heard the initial and ongoing conversion story of Lee, who went from being a directionless and troubled teen to becoming an imperfect but diligent pillar of faith in his home, ward, and stake. We heard from Nadia, including her conviction that Sunday

School and seminary alone are not enough and that foundational individual and family study in the home are essential. Finally, we heard the voice of the Lord's prophet of the present warning us of challenges ahead but optimistically urging us to strengthen our faith and to deepen our conversion. May we continue to do so, "that [our] joy might be full." In chapter 6, we turn to another source of joy, family Sabbath observance.

QUESTIONS TO ENCOURAGE CONTEMPLATION AND CONVERSATION

1. If you could give one piece of advice to a person or family who is struggling with the new home-centered, Church-supported approach to gospel learning and *Come, Follow Me* efforts, what would it be?

2. What counsel or advice shared by members in this chapter did you most appreciate? Why? How might you apply their advice in a helpful way?

3. Nadia, who served as an early-morning seminary teacher and a Young Women's leader in her ward, expressed her opinion that even her best efforts "will not be enough" for most of the youth she has taught, unless they are getting significant foundational gospel teaching at home and through their own personal study. Do you agree? What are the implications for your life if she is correct?

4. Lee, who works in a maximum-security prison, said, "There is enough bad influence out there in the world. . . . We don't need to have it in here . . . , within the walls of our home. The walls of our home should be a sanctuary." How can your family make your home less like the world and more like a sanctuary?

5. President Nelson has said, "I am . . . not naive about the days ahead. . . . If we are to have any hope of sifting through the myriad of voices and the philosophies of men that attack truth, we must learn to receive revelation." How does this direction relate to your life? How does it reflect a keen awareness of families like Nadia and Lee's—and yours?

CREATING OPPORTUNITIES FOR REVELATORY EXPERIENCES (CORE)

1. What intentions do you have to enjoy personal revelatory experiences?
2. How can you and your loved ones encourage each other's revelatory experiences?

3. What personal and relational activities might encourage your own revelatory experiences?

NOTES

1. Ralph Waldo Emerson, "Quotes," Goodreads, https://www.goodreads.com/quotes/19755-that-which-we-persist-in-doing-becomes-easier-to-do.
2. All names are pseudonyms to protect identities.
3. Russell M. Nelson, "Revelation for the Church, Revelation for Our Lives," *Ensign*, May 2018, 96.

CHAPTER SIX

Joyful, Home-Centered Family Sabbath Observance

> *I promise that as you diligently work to remodel your home into a center of gospel learning, over time your Sabbath days will truly be a delight.*
>
> —Russell M. Nelson, "Becoming Exemplary Latter-day Saints"

> *As individuals and families engage in . . . personal worship, and joyful family time, the Sabbath day will truly be a delight.*
>
> —Quentin L. Cook, "Deep and Lasting Conversion to Heavenly Father and the Lord Jesus Christ"

In previous chapters, we heard the voice of our present prophet warning us of challenges ahead while optimistically urging us to strengthen our faith and to deepen our conversion through individual and family gospel study and worship. An additional prophetic priority in recent years has been to urge deeper conversion through joyful, home-centered Sabbath observance. In this chapter, we examine this invitation and explore how some exemplary families model it. We devote most of the chapter to an in-depth exploration of the ways that our Jewish friends observe the Sabbath (*Shabbat*). Then we ask some questions to encourage consideration of how readers might observe joyful Sabbath practices. In the following chapter, we address ways that careful, joyful practice of the *Come, Follow Me* approach can be a blessing for Latter-day Saint families.

The Prophet Joseph Smith taught, "One of the grand fundamental principles of Mormonism is to receive truth, let it come from whence it may."[1] While we should cherish the guidance we receive from our own religious beliefs, scriptures, and Church leaders, we also can benefit from welcoming virtuous direction, inspiration, and comfort from many different sources. In speaking about our friends of other faiths, President Gordon B. Hinckley stated, "Look for their strengths and their virtues, and you will find strength and virtues that will be helpful in your own life."[2]

As keeping the Sabbath day holy has become a profound point of emphasis over the past few years, Apostles have repeatedly pointed to our religiously observant[3] Jewish brothers and sisters as a model of "delighting in the Sabbath." Notably, in a 2015 general conference address, Elder Quentin L. Cook recalled the Jewish Sabbath celebration he and his wife, Mary, attended in the home of their Jewish friends Robert and Diane Abrams. Elder Cook said of this experience,

> It began by blessing the family and singing a Sabbath hymn. . . . The most poignant scriptures read . . . were from Isaiah, declaring the Sabbath a delight, and from Ezekiel, that the Sabbath "shall be a sign between me and you, that ye may know that I am the Lord your God."
>
> The overwhelming impression from this wonderful evening was of family love, devotion, and accountability to God.[4]

So positive was this experience for the Cooks that there seemed to be more than a spark of what has been called "holy envy"[5] regarding this beautiful Jewish celebration of the Sabbath.

In this chapter we will not make extensive connections between how Jewish families observe Shabbat and how Latter-day Saint families might observe the Sabbath. This is because Sabbath observance is unique across families and cultures and because we prefer not to be prescriptive about something so sacred and unique. We invite our readers to consider and to converse as families about how they might enhance joyful Sabbath observance in their current situations.

JEWISH OBSERVANCE OF THE SABBATH

Our Jewish friends have millennia of Sabbath observance to draw from. Jewish authors have written many books and thousands of articles on Shabbat (a Google search of "Shabbat" returned more than nineteen million results). We have space to mention only some of the highlights and to mention only a few sources in the endnotes. In several publications written both to our fellow members of The Church of Jesus Christ of Latter-day Saints[6] and to broader audiences,[7] we are on record as holding a great deal of "holy envy" for how our Jewish friends observe the Sabbath as well as other aspects of Jewish practice.

From the ancient empires of Egypt, Babylon, and Rome to the more recent Holocaust, Jews have been attacked, persecuted, disenfranchised, and banished from society. They have experienced devastating pogroms, had their synagogues burned and bombed, and been expelled from society in many other ways. Through all this, observant Jews have remembered and honored the Sabbath day. We can learn much from them and their dedication to this holy day.

Sabbath observance was one of the Ten Commandments given at Sinai and includes the injunction to "remember the sabbath day, to keep it holy. . . . The seventh day is the sabbath unto the Lord thy God: in it thou shalt not do any work" (Exodus 20:8, 10). Incorporating the divine into weekly Shabbat observance is key for many observant Jewish families. In her book on Jewish family life, Blu Greenberg stated:

> Shabbat in a traditional Jewish household . . . comes fifty-two times more often than any other special day in a Jew's life. As such, it occupies, preoccupies, and marks our lives in ways more pervasive and

more encompassing than one would ever imagine. Although we are often not conscious of it ourselves, our very lives revolve around Shabbat, even as we throw ourselves with full energy into the weekday world.[8]

The Friday evening Shabbat ritual held by observant Jews is among the most ancient continuing weekly family religious practices. The Jewish Sabbath begins at sundown on Friday evening and continues until sundown on Saturday evening. It has been argued that the practice of Shabbat is a reason that Jewish families have remained strong despite repeated anti-Semitic efforts to destroy Judaism and the Jewish people. Indeed, among Jews there is a saying that "more than Jews have kept Shabbat, Shabbat has kept the Jews."[9]

Shabbat (also *Shabbos* or *Sabbath*), meaning "rest" in Hebrew, is the seventh day of the week. In the sacred Jewish text of Genesis, God labored for six days or "times" to create the world. On the seventh day, God rested and marked that day as holy. According to Jewish scripture, God commanded the Israelites to refrain from working on the seventh day. Since antiquity, many Sabbath laws, observances, and traditions have developed under the role of rabbinic authority, including lighting candles, making *challah* (braided bread), studying *Torah* (scripture), singing *zemiroth* (religious songs), praying, blessing children, and eating special Shabbat foods.[10] Typically on Friday just before sundown, Shabbat is ushered in by women (often the mothers of the family) who light two candles and say prayers and blessings. Many Jewish families also have a *Havdalah* ceremony to end the Sabbath,[11] when the father lights a Havdalah braided candle and says four blessings.[12]

In his book *The Sabbath*, Jewish scholar Abraham Joshua Heschel writes, "Judaism is a *religion of time* aiming at *the sanctification of time*." He continues, "Judaism teaches us to be attached to *holiness in time*," and he refers to the Sabbath as a *"palace in time."* Heschel also indicates that after creating the earth, God chose to sanctify time—the seventh day or Sabbath—rather than space (for example, this mountain, that valley, the sun, or the moon). Heschel writes, "Six days a week we wrestle with the world, wringing profit from the earth; on the Sabbath we especially care for the seed of eternity planted in the soul."[13] Others have referred to the Sabbath as a temple in time or as an island of sacred time in a sea of secularism. Given the spiritual rest available within its sacred walls, we could think of the temple as a "Sabbath in space."

There are interesting parallels here to President Nelson's plea for families to transform their homes into a sanctuary of faith and the associated promises and blessings President Nelson identified:

> The new home-centered, Church-supported integrated curriculum has the potential to unleash the power of families, as each family follows through conscientiously and carefully to transform their home into a sanctuary of faith. I promise that as you diligently work to remodel your home into a center of gospel learning, over time *your* Sabbath days will truly be a delight. *Your* children will be excited to learn and to live the Savior's teachings, and the influence of the adversary in *your* life and in *your* home will decrease. Changes in your family will be dramatic and sustaining.[14]

OUR INTERVIEWS WITH JEWISH FAMILIES

For twenty years, we have had the joy of interviewing and learning from more than two hundred diverse families for the American Families of Faith Project[15]—thirty of these have been observant Jewish families. One of the many strengths and virtues of observant Jewish families is the way they strive to keep the Sabbath by making it a joyous holy day. We were sufficiently impressed by what they taught us about the meaning and activities of Shabbat that we published an article referring to Shabbat as "the weekly family ritual par excellence."[16]

Like Elder Cook, we confess admiration for how our Jewish friends observe the Sabbath, but neither we nor Elder Cook are alone in our respect and admiration. In a BYU class we teach called "Family Life in World Religions,"[17] we read a book called *How to Run a Traditional Jewish Household* by Blu Greenberg, an Orthodox Jewish wife and mother. She teaches that the Sabbath is a joyous holy day and that "ordinary experiences often become sublime, because of the special aura created by Shabbat."[18] Many of our BYU students are inspired[19] with how observant Jewish families combine the seemingly disparate processes of both avoiding activities that are fine on other days but not the Sabbath and engaging in unique activities that help make the Sabbath day joyous and spiritual. Some of these differences involve the use of technology and media.

A FEW NOTES ON ELECTRONICS AND THE SABBATH

BYU professors Sarah Coyne and Laura Padilla-Walker are preeminent scholars of how media and technology influence children and families. Their recent review of scores of related studies on media use in families discussed the ways that media can facilitate family connections and enjoyment. However, they also discussed two disturbing realities: First, thirteen- to eighteen-year-old youth are, on average, engaging in nearly nine hours of electronic media time *per day* (six hours for eight- to twelve-year-olds).[20] Second, many relationships are harmed by misuse or overuse of electronic devices. So prevalent is this relational damage and interference that it has been named "technoference."[21] How does this relate to the Sabbath?

One of our Orthodox Jewish colleagues wrote to us a few years ago:

> Our [electronic] devices are so addictive, that some Orthodox young people are having a hard time turning off their phones on Shabbat, to the concern of their elders. . . . One of the key healing functions of Shabbat in our era for observant Jews is that devices (phones, computers, tablets, etc.) are turned off for the full duration of Shabbat. This is crucial to the sanctity and peace of the day. . . . Shabbat offers a day of rest to the brain as well as the soul.

Note the similarity between the spirit of this reflection from our Orthodox Jewish friend and the concerns of President Nelson noted by Elder Cook:

> In addition to encouraging a loving atmosphere in the home, President Nelson has focused on limiting media use that disrupts our primary purposes. One adjustment that will benefit almost any family is to make the internet, social media, and television a servant instead of a distraction or, even worse, a master. The war for the souls of all, but particularly children, is often [fought] in the home. As parents we need

to make sure that media content is wholesome, age appropriate, and consistent with the loving atmosphere we are trying to create.[22]

For prophets and apostles, it seems that the quality of media used is of at least as much concern as the quantity.

The effort to place electronic media and devices in the "servant" role instead of the "master" role is a vital one throughout the week, but it has particular importance on the Sabbath. All of us can bless our families and the rising generations through prayerful self-examination and conversation on this issue. To borrow the ancient Greek philosopher Socrates's phrase, "The unexamined life is not worth living."[23]

INSIGHTS ON THE SABBATH FROM JEWISH YOUTH AND FAMILIES

Indeed, intentionality and focus are of central importance in sacred study, learning, and Sabbath worship for members of our faith and for our Jewish friends. We now shift from the wisdom of intentionally keeping technology in the "servant" position to other Sabbath-related points worthy of our consideration and efforts. Three Orthodox Jewish young adults we interviewed with their parents offered their perspective of Shabbat:

> **Josiah (nineteen-year-old son):** For me, Shabbat is the pinnacle of everything. . . . We all spend time together. We have three meals together. We play [games].
>
> **Nate (twenty-year-old son):** I don't know if there's any particular practice . . . that's . . . more meaningful than [Shabbat] to me personally.
>
> **Zvi (twenty-year-old son):** Shabbat has always been the thing that I keep doing for the family's sake, because whether or not I care about it for religious purposes, it's such a big deal on a family level that that's not something you can cut out.

These three emerging adults emphasized that they valued Shabbat because it provided opportunities for them to spend time together with their families—even though it cost them their electronic devices for a day.

An Orthodox Jewish mother, Mara, stated:

> I like family togetherness. And I think that one of the only ways to achieve that, given the lifestyle of most Americans, is if one can focus on a particular time, a particular holiday, and use those as a vehicle to explore the holiday, to explore the tradition, and to explore each other, and to be with each other. So I value buying into Shabbat and the holy days as a way to bring us closer together.

An Orthodox Jewish couple, Alissa and Yigal, related their Shabbat traditions of unplugging, singing, and dancing with their children:

> **Alissa:** For sure, Shabbat observance [is meaningful to us].... We light Shabbat candles, and we are not on the computer, and we don't drive anywhere. [We] don't talk on the phone or go shopping or do weekly things, and that is very important personally and as a couple.... Now that our older daughter is bigger, we incorporated singing together on Shabbat.... Recently we had friends over, and we all started singing together, and they said, "We don't sing well." But all of us are tone deaf.... [The quality of the singing is not] the issue. It['s] ... the energy. Singing religious songs is really significant to me.
>
> **Yigal:** Definitely singing together is important.... Also, another thing is kind of minor, but [it] is really beautiful.... On Friday night, right after we light candles, we create a little dance with our kids and us. We dance for a minute or two while singing Shabbat songs. They love to do it, and it's such a good thing. There are so many reasons why we love [our Shabbat dance]. Number one, we love it because we made it up.... So that is why I love the dancing[24]—because it's something that we love doing and our children love doing. It injects our Judaism and our family with a sense of joy with the traditions.

Another Jewish mother and father explained:

Linda: [Shabbat] brings you to the closeness of the marriage and the family, things like lighting Shabbat candles or being together during Shabbat. During Shabbat you . . . get that special feeling, . . . that kind of closeness, that sense of unity.

Saul: There's a special meaning to Sabbath traditions when you're doing it [as] a family.

For these families, Shabbat is not somber but is a true delight. Candles, prayers, food, music, dancing, and singing breathe life and energy into their Sabbath worship.

In addition to the sacred but joyous reverie, another meaningful Shabbat practice mentioned by several participants was children's blessings. Few rituals capture and reflect the passing on of an intergenerational legacy of faith and the deeply held Jewish value of *v'shinantam l'vanecha* ("You shall teach your children") as richly as the Shabbat blessings of children by their parents. Indeed, Shabbat can be thought of as an intergenerational chain going back through history.

During the blessing, after placing hands on the head of the child, the parent speaks the following words (typically in Hebrew):

- For boys, the introductory statement is "May you be like Ephraim and Manasseh."
- For girls, the introductory statement is "May you be like Sarah, Rebecca, Rachel, and Leah."

For both boys and girls, the rest of the formal blessing consists of the words of the priestly blessing that God commanded Aaron and his descendants to speak to the people of Israel:

The Lord bless thee, and keep thee;

The Lord make His face shine upon thee, and be gracious unto thee;

The Lord lift up His countenance upon thee, and give thee peace. (Numbers 6:24–26)[25]

In traditional (Orthodox) Jewish families, typically only the father blesses the children, while in more progressive families (Reform, Conservative), fathers or mothers or both bless their children. Here is how one popular Jewish website describes blessing children:

> The blessing is performed differently in every family. In some traditional homes, only the father blesses the children. In other families, both parents give blessings—either together and in unison, or first one parent, followed by the other. In some homes the mother blesses the girls and the father blesses the boys.
>
> Usually the person giving the blessing places one or both hands on the child's head. Some parents bless each child in succession, working from oldest to youngest. Others bless all of the girls together, and all of the boys together.
>
> After the blessing, some parents take a moment to whisper something to their child—praising him or her for something he or she did during the week, or conveying some extra encouragement and love. Almost every family concludes the blessing with a kiss or a hug.[26]

Several parents that we interviewed established traditions in their homes of blessing their children on the Sabbath, as illustrated by the comment from the following Reform couple:

David: We [specially] bless the kids . . . on Friday nights.

Rebecca: The blessings that we do on Friday night . . . I never even knew existed as a child. It is a special time when the parents bless the children. It is a beautifully wonderful and tender moment that we have really come to [love] and our children have come to expect. [It's] not just that we put our hands on their heads and bless them. . . . Each of us says something to each child about something that we're proud of that they've done this week. [The Shabbat blessing is] just a wonderful thing that . . . we didn't make that up. . . . If we just look at what our tradition teaches us, it was already there. Jewish parents have been doing that for thousands of years.

Another Reform Jewish couple discussed Shabbat blessings of their children in detail:

Scott: Most Friday nights we do a blessing with the kids. [We] bless them and whisper what they did good for the week in their ear, and they look forward to that.

Julie: In . . . the Torah, there's a blessing. . . . It's a blessing in Hebrew, but it [says], "May God bless you and keep you. May his light shine upon you and be gracious unto you." It's the priestly benediction, so we say that blessing, and then we do whisper something [extra] in each of their ears. . . . It's [often] some kindness that [they] did. It's to [help them] . . . always remember that the things that we told them that we were proud of them for were . . . acts that God would be proud of you [for]—how you acted to somebody else [with] kindness [and] honesty . . .

Scott: Now they look forward to it. I think if it was just a blessing, they wouldn't care.

Julie: So the [extra] thing that we whisper in their ear is not like "Oh, I'm so glad you made an A on the spelling test"; it's some kindness that [they] did. . . . So you don't have to be a great athlete or a great student; it's [about] just being a good person. . . .

It's funny, because [one of our sons] is really serious about what we whisper in his ear, and if you whisper something vague [or] general, like "I'm really proud of how you were nice to your brother this week," then he'll say, "Like when?" . . . You can't get away with [it] if you didn't pay attention that week to something. It really takes a lot of work to have something [specific to say]. So [you try to] . . . catch them being really good.

For Rebecca and David, for Scott and Julie, there seems to be a sacred but also pronounced child-centric emphasis with Shabbat. Their emphasis on speaking repeatedly to children about what they are proud of them for echoes the way that Heavenly Father, whenever He speaks of the Savior, says, "This is my beloved son, in whom I am well pleased" (Matthew 3:17; see also Matthew 17:5; 3 Nephi 11:7).

What does the reverence of Shabbat mean for children in such families? One young woman from another family explained the following:

> **Hannah (seventeen-year-old Conservative Jewish daughter):** The rest of the week [is a] totally different time. [When] we have Shabbat . . . [it is] different. We don't have to worry about the rest of the world. The rest of the world goes on, but we are here with our family and our religion. That's just . . . it's our time.

Note the demarcation of both time and space in Hannah's description: there is "the rest of the week" and there is "the rest of the world," but on Shabbat, Hannah explains, "We are here with our family and our religion. . . . It's our time." With three "our" references in one quote, Hannah places her own adolescent stamp of familial "we-ness" and unity on Shabbat. A Conservative Jewish mother named Sarah shared the following:

> When we take the time out, when we light the candles Friday night, that's a time that I feel really close to [my children]. . . . When we sit across the table from each other, my husband and I, and the Sabbath candles are lit, and I see the kids, there is something I get from that that is *so deep*. It's just a feeling that [all is right in the world]. . . . It doesn't matter what else is going on. Right in that circle . . . it's awe-inspiring.

Sarah's husband, Daniel, later emphasized, "I don't know that the Sabbath meal is a religious experience for most people, but for me it's the heart of religion."

For Sarah and Daniel, "the heart of their religion beats strongest not in the synagogue, but around their family dinner table—which according to Jewish tradition represents a sacred altar, a place of communion between God and His children."[27]

Many participants commented on how religious observance and rituals contributed to the success of their marriage, including a Jewish mother named Asha, who discussed the role of ritual and sacred routine. In response to the question "Are there ways that your religious beliefs or practices help you to avoid or reduce marital conflict?" Asha responded,

> The first thing that comes to mind is the routine. And another thing that I've come to understand and believe is that religious belief and truly religious moments don't just come from . . . nowhere. One has to be in the habit of religious practice and religious observance. . . . If you wait for the mood to hit you, it never will. But if you go, if you observe, if you practice on a regular . . . basis, then you're open to God. . . .
>
> I think that our routine of going to synagogue every week, that it is something we do whether we really feel like it or not. . . . It is what we chose to do. It's about the Sabbath. It's what you do on the Sabbath. It is such a calming experience when tensions are high, when frustration is high.

For Asha, the Sabbath was a "calming experience." For a husband named Israel, "the rules" of Jewish tradition reportedly helped him and his wife avoid conflict. He explained:

> Things that might have been conflicts before aren't even issues, because we know the rules. What are we doing on Saturday? Well, that's not an issue. Where and what are we eating? It's not an issue. . . . This is the way it is. I want to go [somewhere, so] we look at the calendar. "Oh no, we can't go here because it's yom tov, it's a holiday," [but] it's . . . OK. It's not a conflict [between us]. These are not issues, because there's a higher authority that we all are agreed with. That's our priority.

Religious observance not only influenced marriage; such efforts also facilitated peaceful parent-child relationships.[28] One mother, Lila, explained, "[Talking] about Jewish values as a family . . . Shabbat . . . pausing and coming together . . . [helps us] when conflict arises, because we are all there . . . together as a family."

Shabbat traditions like eating family meals, playing games, singing, and blessing the children are (at their best) special, even sacred. In the words of Blu Greenberg,

> There is something . . . about the power of habit and routine. . . . There are some things that spontaneity simply cannot offer—a steadiness and stability which, at its very least, has the emotional reward of familiarity, and at best, creates the possibility of investing time with special meaning, experience with special value, and life with a moment of transcendence.[29]

WHAT WE CAN LEARN FROM OUR JEWISH FRIENDS[30]

The Lord desires that we "call the sabbath a delight, the holy of the Lord" (Isaiah 58:13). He invites (even commands) us to keep the Sabbath "with a glad heart and a cheerful countenance" (Doctrine and Covenants 59:15). The words "delight" and "glad" and "cheerful" suggest to us that the Lord views Sabbath observance as a path toward spiritual joy and pleasure and that He desires for us to approach Sabbath observance with an attitude of delightful enjoyment. Elder Quentin L. Cook has noted that

> a most remarkable change has occurred in the Church. This has been in the response of the members to renewed emphasis on the Sabbath by . . . President Russell M. Nelson's challenge to make the Sabbath a delight. Many members understand that truly keeping the Sabbath day holy is a refuge from the storms of this life. It is also a sign of our devotion to our Father in Heaven and an increased understanding of the sacredness of sacrament meeting. . . . We have a long way to go, but we have a wonderful beginning.[31]

Members of The Church of Jesus Christ of Latter-day Saints can learn from their Jewish friends about how to make the Sabbath a delight by unitedly choosing ways to make it special, joyous, spiritual, and peaceful. Of course, each family will choose the ways they feel they can best make the Sabbath a delight.

In the next chapter, we will hear testimonies from an array of members of the Church of Jesus Christ regarding how specific prophetic promises are being fulfilled in their personal and family lives. Fittingly, one of those promises is that our "Sabbath days will be a delight."[32]

QUESTIONS TO ENCOURAGE CONTEMPLATION AND CONVERSATION

1. Each week Orthodox Jews take a one-day break from electronic devices to focus solely on faith and family without distraction. How might doing likewise enrich our own church and family worship, our level of sacred focus, and our depth of relationships?

2. To help make the Sabbath an "island of sacred time" and a respite from the "wrestle with the world," on that day observant Jews do not discuss "the cares of the world," including money, business, or related concerns. This allows time, energy, and focus to discuss heavenly, eternal, and spiritual things that bring deeper delight. The Book of Mormon states that "we talk of Christ, we rejoice in Christ" (2 Nephi 25:26). How can Latter-day Saint families make the Sabbath a delight as they rejoice in Christ by talking of His life, miracles, Atonement, and Resurrection?

3. Jewish families often share the Sabbath by inviting guests. One way for Latter-day Saint families to make the Sabbath a delight is to invite others into their homes. Inviting those of our family and friends—Latter-day Saint friends and friends of other faiths—who would be particularly blessed by being with an active Latter-day Saint family on the Sabbath is especially delightful. These gatherings could include shared participation in *Come, Follow Me*. How else might Latter-day Saint families invite others to share the Sabbath with them?

4. Jewish women usher in Shabbat on Friday just before sundown by lighting two candles. As part of this tradition, a Jewish wife solemnly prays for the Jewish temple to be rebuilt and prays for family members. To end the Sabbath, Jewish men say the Havdalah blessings, which includes praying for the spirit of the Sabbath to linger throughout the week. We can make the Sabbath a delight by praying about things that matter most, including praying that the joyful spirit of the Sabbath day can remain throughout the

week. How might we work together so that both husbands and wives, as equal partners, can do their part to make the Sabbath a delight?

5. Like our Jewish brothers and sisters, we can learn that the Sabbath is the perfect time to bless our children literally and figuratively and to celebrate our shared walk of faith. What are ways for children to hear their mother and father pray to our Heavenly Father for them? (see 3 Nephi 19:23). What are ways to facilitate children (of any age) receiving more fathers' blessings?

6. Our Jewish friends celebrate both the creation of the earth and the redemption from slavery on the Sabbath. As members of the Church of Jesus Christ, how can we better rejoice in the Lord and celebrate our redemption from death and sin on the Sabbath?

7. Across many generations and many cultures, the ancestors of our Jewish friends have been persecuted and killed. Despite this, or perhaps because of this, our Jewish friends frequently say, with gusto, the Hebrew phrase *l'chaim!* ("To life!"). They take extra care on the Sabbath day to celebrate life—particularly a life devoted to worshipping God and binding couples and families together in and through that worship. How can we better celebrate the sacred and familial joy of life?

CREATING OPPORTUNITIES FOR REVELATORY EXPERIENCES (CORE)

1. What intentions do you have to enjoy personal revelatory experiences?
2. How can you and your loved ones encourage each other's revelatory experiences?
3. What personal and relational activities might encourage your own revelatory experiences?

NOTES

1. Joseph Smith, "History, 1838–1856, volume E-1 [1 July 1843–30 April 1844]," p. 1666, The Joseph Smith Papers, https://www.josephsmithpapers.org/paper-summary/history-1838-1856-volume-e-1-1-july-1843-30-april-1844/36.
2. Quoted in Sheri L. Dew, *Go Forward with Faith: The Biography of Gordon B. Hinckley* (Salt Lake City: Deseret Book, 1996), 576.
3. The term "observant" is used in Judaism to mean those who observe the commandments and religious expectations such as daily prayer, keeping kosher, keeping the Sabbath holy, and so forth.

4. Quentin L. Cook, "Shipshape and Bristol Fashion: Be Temple Worthy—in Good Times and Bad Times," *Ensign*, November 2015, 41.
5. Loren D. Marks and David C. Dollahite, "Surmounting the Empathy Wall: Deep Respect and Holy Envy in Qualitative Scholarship," *Marriage & Family Review* 54, no. 7 (2018): 762–73.
6. See David C. Dollahite and Loren D. Marks, "Jewish Families: How Teachings and Traditions Strengthen Marriage and Family Life," *Public Square*, September 14, 2021, https://publicsquaremag.org/faith/jewish-families-how-teachings-and-traditions-strengthen-marriage-and-family-life/; and Dollahite and Marks, "Approaching God: Jewish and Latter-day Saint Prayer and Worship," in *"The Learning of the Jews": What Latter-day Saints Can Learn from Jewish Religious Experience*, ed. Trevan G. Hatch and Leonard J. Greenspoon (Salt Lake City: Greg Kofford Books, 2021), 115–41.
7. See David C. Dollahite, Trevan G. Hatch, and Loren D. Marks, "Relational Implications of Jewish Family Ritual and Practice," in *Routledge Handbook of Jewish Ritual and Practice*, ed. Oliver Leaman (New York: Routledge, forthcoming).
8. Blu Greenberg, *How to Run a Traditional Jewish Household* (New York: Simon and Schuster, 1985), 93–94.
9. Ahad Ha'am first said this, but it has been widely discussed and debated among Jews. Indeed, a Google search for that phrase returned more than 1.9 million responses. See Amy Kalmanofsky, "Kept by Shabbat," March 2, 2018, in *JTS Torah Commentary*, podcast, https://www.jtsa.edu/torah/kept-by-shabbat/.
10. See Trevan Hatch and Loren Marks, "Judaism and Orthodox Judaism," in *The Social History of the American Family*, ed. Marilyn J. Coleman and Lawrence H. Ganong (Thousand Oaks, CA: SAGE, 2014), 781.
11. There are some important differences among the three major branches of Judaism in how the Sabbath is observed. For example, while an Orthodox family would view Shabbat as a *chiyuv*, or nonnegotiable obligation, a Reform or Conservative family might be more flexible and negotiate around events and conflicts that arise from secular culture.
12. On Shabbat being ushered in by women and ushered out by men, see Chaya M. Klein, "The Three Mitzvot of the Woman," https://www.mikvah.org/article/the_three_mitzvot_of_the_woman; and Nechoma Greisman and Chana Ne'eman, "Ushering Shabbat In," https://www.chabad.org/library/article_cdo/aid/78057/jewish/Ushering-Shabbat-In.htm.
13. Abraham Joshua Heschel, *The Sabbath: Its Meaning for Modern Man* (New York: Farrar, Straus and Giroux, 2000), 13; emphasis in original.
14. Russell M. Nelson, "Becoming Exemplary Latter-day Saints," *Ensign*, November 2018, 113.
15. "American Families of Faith Project," School of Family Life, Brigham Young University, https://americanfamiliesoffaith.byu.edu/.
16. Loren D. Marks, Trevan G. Hatch, and David C. Dollahite, "Sacred Practices and Family Processes in a Jewish Context: Shabbat as the Weekly Family Ritual Par Excellence," *Family Process* 57, no. 2 (2017): 448–61.
17. Dave designed and teaches this course, and Loren has been a substitute instructor for it.
18. Greenberg, *Traditional Jewish Household*, 28.
19. See David C. Dollahite, "Holy Envy: What We Learn by Studying Other Faiths," RealClearReligion, May 4, 2020, https://www.realclearreligion.org/articles/2020/05/04/holy_envy_what_we_learn_by_studying_other_faiths_490589.html.

20. Laura M. Padilla-Walker, Sarah M. Coyne, and Madison K. Memmott-Elison, "Media and the Family," in *APA Handbook of Contemporary Family Psychology*, ed. Barbara H. Fiese, vol. 2, *Applications and Broad Impact of Family Psychology* (Washington, DC: American Psychological Association, 2019), 365–78.
21. Padilla-Walker, Coyne, and Memmott-Elison, "Media and the Family," 368.
22. Quentin L. Cook, "Great Love for Our Father's Children," *Ensign*, May 2019, 79.
23. This phrase is recorded in Plato, *Apology of Socrates*, 38a.
24. Typically, a Jewish dance is a circle dance that involves holding hands.
25. Quoted from *The Holy Scriptures according to the Masoretic Text*, vol. 1 (Philadelphia: Jewish Publication Society of America, 1966). Verse 27 states, "So shall they put My name upon the children of Israel, and I will bless them."
26. Tamar Fox, "Blessing the Children," My Jewish Learning, https://www.myjewish learning.com/article/blessing-the-children/.
27. Loren D. Marks and David C. Dollahite, "'Don't Forget Home': The Importance of Sacred Ritual in Families," in *Understanding Religious Rituals*, ed. John P. Hoffman (New York: Routledge, 2012), 195.
28. In several recent articles we have discussed ways that religious parents can approach religious practices in ways that are positive, harmonious, and healthy: David C. Dollahite, Loren D. Marks, and Hal Boyd, "The Best Practices—and Benefits—of Religious Parenting," *Public Discourse*, February 6, 2020, https://www.thepublicdiscourse .com/2020/02/59688/; Betsy Hughes Barrow, David C. Dollahite, and Loren D. Marks, "How Parents Balance Desire for Religious Continuity with Honoring Children's Religious Agency," *Psychology of Religion and Spirituality* 13, no. 2 (2021): 222–34; David C. Dollahite and Loren D. Marks, "Positive Youth Religious and Spiritual Development: What We Have Learned from Religious Families," *Religions* 10, no. 10 (2019): 548; and David C. Dollahite et al., "Beyond Religious Rigidities: Religious Firmness and Religious Flexibility as Complementary Loyalties in Faith Transmission," *Religions* 10, no. 2 (2019): 111.
29. Greenberg, *Traditional Jewish Household*, 27–28.
30. In this section, we draw from David C. Dollahite and Loren Marks, "Making the Sabbath a Delight: Seven Lessons from Strong Jewish Families," *Meridian*, February 23, 2018, https://ldsmag.com/making-the-sabbath-a-delight-seven-lessons-from-strong -jewish-families/; and David C. Dollahite, "Sabbath Observance: Families Can Learn to Make the Sabbath 'a Delight,'" *Church News*, December 23, 2015, https://www .thechurchnews.com/archives/2015-12-23/sabbath-observance-families-can-learn -to-make-the-sabbath-a-delight-29143.
31. Cook, "Shipshape and Bristol Fashion," 42.
32. Nelson, "Becoming Exemplary Latter-day Saints," 113.

CHAPTER SEVEN

Fulfillment of Prophetic Promises

We begin this chapter not with the prophet but with a Pulitzer Prize winner. The prize-winning author and psychiatrist Robert Coles has observed that truly great literature is precious—not primarily because such a work entertains readers but because it issues an implicit yet irrepressible moral call to them to be better than they were before encountering the book.[1]

The Lord has issued His own call to us to diligently seek "out of the best books words of wisdom . . . , even by study and also by faith" (Doctrine and Covenants 88:118). Our prophets have taught that the scriptures stand at the head of those great books and that, in the case of the Book of Mormon, we will "get nearer to God by abiding by its precepts, than by any other book."[2] This encouraging promise of power, rooted in responding to the call of seeking learning out of the best books, continues through the prophet of our day.

In his concluding October 2018 general conference address, President Russell M. Nelson said, "I promise that as you diligently work to remodel your home into a center of gospel learning, over time [1] *your* Sabbath days will truly be a delight. [2] *Your* children will be excited to learn and to live the Savior's teachings, and [3] the influence of the adversary in *your* life and in *your* home will decrease."[3]

In the *Come, Follow Me* survey, we asked Church members the question "Have any of these [prophetic promises] been fulfilled for you and your family?" We are profoundly grateful to the members of stake presidencies and councils and the hundreds of other members (in two US states) who invested time and effort in sharing information that we hope will be instructive for many members.

A few responses to our question about the fulfillment of prophetic promises were antagonistic or negative. Others acknowledged challenges with humor, such as one sister who wrote, "The most challenging part is understanding what we are reading. Especially the writings of Paul. Bless him, but he is difficult to understand sometimes!" Despite the array of real challenges among them, most of those who had not yet seen the prophetic promises fulfilled seemed to feel a genuine longing to improve gospel learning as individuals and families so that they *would* realize and claim the promised blessings. We now turn to many accounts that acknowledged fulfilled promises.

PROPHETIC PROMISES FULFILLED: PERSONAL AND FAMILY ACCOUNTS

Based on reports from women and men, empty nesters and younger folks, singles and marrieds, many had seen President Nelson's prophetic promises begin to be realized in their lives. In fact, the reports were numerous enough that we will seek to share them using the categories outlined by President Nelson in the quote at the beginning of this chapter. We first cover President Nelson's promise about the Sabbath.

PROMISE 1: "*YOUR* SABBATH DAYS WILL TRULY BE A DELIGHT"

As diverse members addressed how and whether their efforts to respond to the *Come, Follow Me* invitation have made their Sabbath days more of a delight, they shared the following brief but encouraging responses:

"I find it easier to keep the Sabbath."

"Our Sabbath days have definitely been better! It has been easier to choose to follow the gospel and keep my Sabbath days holy."

"We spend much, much more time studying the gospel and working together than before [with *Come, Follow Me*]."

"The Sabbath day has become more of a delight."

One young husband, a university student, wrote, "My wife and I still do not have children; however, our Sabbath days have been more delightful. Being consistent with *Come, Follow Me* has increased our knowledge. . . . We have [even] eliminated doing any activities such as homework that would detract."

A parent with several children wrote, "The Sabbath is becoming a true day for gospel study, resting, and spending time with family. It's not as much of a rush but really a delight. Though we are not perfect at studying throughout the week, we love being on the same study topic with our kids and having discussions with even our younger kids." One member wrote, "I certainly don't dread church anymore. . . . The curriculum has been [a] good [change]."

There were some concerns voiced, however. One parent in a challenging home situation wrote, "I feel more isolated from the ward and miss the third hour. I spend enough time with my family and have heard their experiences and stories many times; I wish I could hear fresh examples and applications from people outside my family. That third hour helped me make more friends, too. Three-hour church was a 'delight' for me."

A young wife without children told us, "The Sabbath day is often a delight. However, as a young married person at church, I often feel disposable and unknown. . . . I know that a lot of young married couples feel this way in our ward."

Increased awareness of needs like those expressed above can help us to better involve and minister to our gospel sisters and brothers and to strive to better fill the hole that the change has left for some.

A parent with children serving in class and quorum presidencies reported that, yes, the prophet's promises "were being fulfilled" and that "Sabbath days are . . . our favorite day" but also said that "we are spread out often as a family on the day due to duties, meetings, visits." The series of meetings could make it difficult to "get a few extra moments at home to reflect." One parent similarly wrote, as reported in an earlier chapter,

> It sometimes feels like we as a church are still trying to have a "Church-centered, family-supported" approach. Especially with teenagers of both genders, there are tons of things that eat into my family's together time, including [ward youth council], fast offerings, ward choir, etc. This, along with the admonitions to be doing more and more things (temple work, family history, missionary service, etc.), has left me feeling a bit burnt out. I feel like I am falling behind, and some days I'm not sure if I will ever be able to catch up. On my worst days, I question if I even want to try.

Vigilant and sensitive Church leaders will take notice of how meetings can be harmonized or minimized to support the family rather than compete with it. We suspect that many, if not most, members have days when burnout seems possible. Ideally, the invitation to "come, follow me" will be a strengthening resource rather than a stressful demand. Perhaps no comment captured the view of *Come, Follow Me* as a recharging and strengthening resource better than the following reflection from a mother who wrote,

> I really treasure the Sabbath day, and I can say it is a delight in our home. As a mother with a full-time job, plus trying to cover all my responsibilities as a mother, wife, grandmother, daughter, and my calling at church, sometimes it can be overloading. But as [I] take time every day not only reading my personal scriptures but also following and study[ing] the new program *Come, Follow Me* with our family, . . . I [get] a recharge[d] spiritual battery.

Several leaders have commented that *Come, Follow Me* is intended to be a blessing, not a burden, but that ideals can be hard to reach. Encouragingly, many parents discussed the closer integration and harmony between gospel learning at home and gospel learning at church. One parent said, "During Sunday dinners, we go around the table, and each person shares something they talked about in their class. It was great to hear the different perspectives each child gained in their classes about the same scriptures."

Another mother reported that

> before the new integrated curriculum was implemented, we studied the scriptures together as a family. But now that our scripture study at home mirrors what our children are hearing in Primary, they are making . . . connections. Sometimes those are as simple as "Hey, we talked about that in our class!" and sometimes they are a little more introspective as they remember what others shared. We hear from their teachers that they are also more willing to participate in the lessons because we have reviewed the stories at home.

Continuing this thought, many members addressed home and church together. Encouraging notes regarding this integration included the following:

> "I [have] loved having the same curriculum used by our children and the adults. It [has] made our family scripture study more relevant as we [are] . . . discussing the same scriptures."

> "I have never gone to church prepared to talk about the lesson or had my own spiritual thoughts, revelations, or promptings prepared to share until this new curriculum. Because of that reason, my Sabbath day observance while in church has become a delight."

> "Since beginning our study with the *Come, Follow Me* program, we've found that the centralized curriculum has helped us have more meaningful gospel discussions in our home and to be better prepared for our Sunday meetings."

"I have seen my Sabbath days become more of a delight as I've come more prepared to Sunday School. I am much more able to focus in class and learn because of using *Come, Follow Me* during the week."

"I teach Sunday School to fourteen- and fifteen-year-olds. I have seen thrilling things happen with those kids as we are teaching their lessons. Just yesterday in our class, one . . . boy mentioned how he had seen the video about the lesson at home with his mother and sister. He accepted the lesson as true because of seminary working on it, Sunday School working on it, and also his good mother working on it. A triple whammy!!!"

"Sabbath days seem more 'delightful,' especially [now] that the teacher, or yourself, [is]n't the only one . . . prepared for enlightening discussions."

Improvements were identified by several members as home and church gospel study efforts better aligned and mutually supported each other.

In summary, President Nelson's first promise to those who "diligently work to remodel [their] home into a center of gospel learning" was that their "Sabbath days will truly be a delight."[4] We anticipated that most member responses would emphasize home-based aspects of this promise, but as evidenced above, many members also experienced a beneficial harmony and synergy between home and church efforts that they greatly appreciated and viewed as blessings. We now turn to President Nelson's second promise.

PROMISE 2: *"YOUR* CHILDREN WILL BE EXCITED TO LEARN AND TO LIVE THE SAVIOR'S TEACHINGS"

In a response that seemed to combine the blessings of the first and second promises, one parent wrote, "[Our] children are more engaged and excited to share what they learned in Sunday classes because of the connection to home study (and vice versa from what their leaders have shared)."

Based on members' reports, this has been the experience for many. However, it appears that children's level of excitement can be largely influenced by whether they are participating in a dialogic discussion (which might excite them) or being preached to (which might bore them). One parent reported, "We fight about how long church at home should be because we have three generations under the same roof, [and] 75 percent [of us have] attention deficit disorder [and] varying attention spans, and [then we have] one person who takes over every discussion and needs to share an example for every point."

The following comments from two different parents urge all parents to preach less and listen more:

> "I have seen in our family a greater desire to study the weekly *Come, Follow Me* agenda, and the Spirit has been stronger when we discuss the new insights we [all] have learned. I have found [that] as we let our daughters talk more about their experiences in the reading, there is more involvement on everyone's part and better discussion."

> "My child knows his scriptures and wants to follow God and make good choices. It's just hard for him to concentrate when [an adult] want[s] two-hour [*Come, Follow Me* in] lecture mode. [My child] needs visuals, questions, and interactive learning. . . . I wish someone at stake conference would say, 'If you have young kids in your home, please make [*Come, Follow Me*] interactive and fun! It's not meant to be a lecture, monologue, or drudgery!' You can have fun while being righteous. Some adults have forgotten this."

Many parents are improving as listeners, facilitators, and discussion leaders while surrendering the predilection for preaching. Many discussion leaders seem to be finding ways to make *Come, Follow Me* engaging and enjoyable. We salute them and hope you will draw some inspiration from their efforts, as we have.

Next, we have opted to offer a substantial series of members' verbatim responses relating to President Nelson's second promise. Reports are presented in a developmental order from families with toddlers to those with adult children.

PARENTS OF TODDLERS

"We love this promise! As we have continued to study, our stubborn toddler who refused to pray has started taking turns praying. She plays going to church, sings primary songs, and shows excitement about scripture study. I'm grateful to start to see her becoming excited about the Savior's teachings. We are going to keep trying so that that trend will continue and increase, and we await the fulfillment of all of these promises as we improve!"

"My daughter is two, and for family home evening every week, we tried to do one of the suggestions from the *Come, Follow Me* manual for that week's material. I think it helped a lot with her coming to know more about who Jesus is and what He has done for all of us."

PARENTS OF PRIMARY-AGE CHILDREN

"We have definitely noticed a difference in our children's excitement to study the teachings found in the scriptures. They are generally excited to open up their scriptures and take turns reading. Our discussions are improving, and they are starting to open up more and share their own thoughts and understanding of what they read."

"I have seen a marked difference in my young children's excitement about the gospel. They look forward to reading either *Come, Follow Me* or the scriptures each night before bed and now remind us if we . . . forget."

PARENTS OF PRETEENS

"My preteen boys now look forward to studying scriptures and the manual with me because the curriculum helps it make more sense to them. It provides order and routine. They enjoy the supplemental materials (videos, etc.) and diverse topics within each lesson. They also now put up a scripture from the lesson on a letter board in our living room that we keep on display all week."

PARENTS OF TEENS

"My seventeen-year-old daughter has always been a challenge to get to read scriptures, [but] this year she has mostly willingly read with us and even reminds us to read."

"My teenage sons have been more interested and excited to learn what *Come, Follow Me* points out . . . that we didn't notice or talk about [on our own]."

"My children live in a world of filth and vulgarity (also known as high school)! While they try to filter it out during the day, I find they come home and are able to articulate their experiences as they relate to being children of God vs. examples of those circumstances around them. It's more than just resisting temptation. From what I see, it is truly learning who they are in contrast with who Satan would have them believe they are. It's a beautiful thing to watch unfold and be a part of."

PARENTS OF CHILDREN OF A VARIETY OF AGES

"My family looks forward to discussions of the lesson with others. My youngest understands and appreciates the Savior more, as [I have] heard in his family and personal prayers."

"My kids like coming together as a family and learning about the Savior. The younger ones are starting to pay more attention, and our home has Christ as [the] focal point."

PARENTS OF ADULT CHILDREN

"Even though our children are grown, I think that all three [promises] are happening in our family. Even our inactive family members have been blessed, because we have received insight into how to stay close to them and help them spiritually."

On the heels of these reports of blessings being received, we remind you of some reported challenges:

"Our four teenagers are not interested . . . [and] push back a lot."

"[I struggle with] not losing my cool when the kids act up."

As social scientists, we have studied religious family practices for twenty-five years. As parents, we have tried to facilitate these practices in our own homes for decades. We have found that studying sacred family practices is often easier than successfully implementing them. We understand, despite the mostly optimistic and positive reports above, that family worship is a labor of love and perseverance. Even in the most successful families, a key recurring feature is a deep commitment to keep trying after failures (including epic failures). In particular, sometimes parents of teens feel that all the work they did during the earlier years is for naught, since many teens become resistant to family religious practices.

We have written to a national audience in the *Atlantic* about home evening and noted elements that can apply equally to *Come, Follow Me*:

> Of course, even the most committed and family-focused Latter-day Saints struggle to make time each week for such a family devotional. Challenges to consistent practice of family home evening include busy schedules, the apathy of teenagers, and the siren call of social media and other entertainment. On the other hand, the stability the practice brings can be just what's needed to counteract those impediments; one mother we interviewed emphasized that it is when life is "craziest" that people need the organizing, calming predictability of family ritual most.[5]

Your next significant home evening or *Come, Follow Me* success may well follow several or even many mediocre (or worse) attempts—but we hope that, like us, you will draw strength from the encouraging reports of our fellow members, including one who noted that, even as imperfect efforts were made, "we have felt a much stronger spirit throughout the week." We again reference Heather Howell Kelley's insight that the joy and benefits of family learning and worship come "not every time, but over time."[6]

Has *Come, Follow Me* yielded the promised blessing that "*your* children will be excited to learn and to live the Savior's teachings"? In many cases, yes. However, most families seem to include at least one child who is not fully responsive to this invitation. Even in that context, however, we can each strive to honor agency, live with charity, and hope and pray for miracles yet to come. We now consider President Nelson's third promised blessing.

PROMISE 3: "THE INFLUENCE OF THE ADVERSARY IN *YOUR* LIFE AND IN *YOUR* HOME WILL DECREASE"

Among the members who reported on the prophet's promised blessings associated with "diligently work[ing] to remodel your home into a center of gospel learning," the responses to the third promise were the most mixed and complex. Perhaps this is because the promise states that the influence of the adversary will *decrease*, not that the influence of the adversary will *cease*.

In connection with the second promise, one mother reported, "My children live in a world of filth and vulgarity (also known as high school)!" We all confront facets of that world of filth and vulgarity—and that world does not disappear when we do *Come, Follow Me*. One parent wrote that in connection with the first promise, "Sundays have improved." With the second promise, yes, the parent's "kids get excited for 'third hour' [at home]." However, the same parent concluded, "[We are] still waiting for the third promise to kick in."

Indeed, the adversary is an impossibly difficult opponent to permanently shake. No group seemed more attuned to or concerned with this reality than the parents of teens. One parent wrote, "Where I am entering a stage in life where my kids are turning into teens, I'll take whatever I can get as far as protection from the adversary." One young parent not currently faced with parenting during the teen years was forward-looking enough that it occupied her thoughts in the present. She explained:

> Although I feel the adversary is working harder and harder to discourage the Lord's faithful people, I know for my family there has been

something different about our home. I feel a greater sense of duty to teach my family so [deeply] that all else is a supplement. We have received blessings as a family currently, and I feel (and am counting on) more blessings on hold for a future day when my children will need them to combat Satan and his efforts. I am confident the learning that's taking place here in our home now will help build a strong foundation for my children when they will need it most later.

"Later" may well be the postteen, emerging adulthood years. Parents can draw some encouragement from the example of Alma the Younger (see Alma 36). The practices and prayers of Alma's father came to fruition later in Alma's life when Alma finally remembered his father sharing teachings about the Savior Jesus Christ. Similarly, Enos needed time to fully process and act on his father's teachings about seeking the Lord (see Enos 1).

However, many have learned that no amount of parental diligence can override a teen's, an emerging adult's, or a later adult's God-given agency to choose otherwise. As we have reported,

> [Hopefully we can find] the sweet spot where parents share their beloved faith through conversation, not preaching, and through authentic modeling and lived example, not coercion. . . .
>
> The irony is that, like any gift, the gift of faith is not always accepted and treasured. We have much to learn in how to offer, receive and reject in ways that are relationally gracious.[7]

It seems that if we are to see the influence of the adversary decrease, it is not enough to teach the Lord's doctrine. We must also strive to teach His doctrine *in the manner and spirit* that He taught it—namely, through word and example, with profound love, with a listening ear, and with respect, even for those who may choose to reject His infinite gift.

When we asked members about the promise that the influence of the adversary in their life and home would decrease, several shifted to a comparative mode in which they contrasted times of success with times of missing home worship and study. One parent wrote, "For our family and myself, the lack of the Spirit and the greater influence of the adversary is always

[a] stunning contrast and result of the lack of consistency and diligence in obeying the prophet's counsel." Framed differently, when the prophet's advice has not been heeded, the influence of the Spirit decreases while the influence of the adversary increases. For this parent, the contrast was "stunning."

Vocalizing a similar study in contrasts, another parent wrote, "There is a stark difference when my husband and I don't utilize *Come, Follow Me* during the week. We feel less safe. . . . [We feel] more stressful influence from the outside world. Less love of God."

A third witness of contrast between the no-effort and higher-effort approach to following the prophet was offered as follows: "I believe any promise that a prophet makes is fulfilled if you keep [your] end of the bargain. My family has not been perfect with using this new curriculum. There is still much we could improve on. However, whenever we do it, we are closer as a family, we are happier, and our spiritual resolve increases."

One member reported that while there were no discernible dramatic changes, "[as] I [do] my own individual reading . . . I do find more worldly media to be offensive and don't have the desire to experience that worldly media."

A parent of teens similarly addressed decreased social media influence as a benefit of personal and family worship: "Being able to spend time discussing doctrine has helped fight a lot of the noise that social media is pressing on our older children."

A wife with an empty nest noted decreased arguments with her husband and other improvements. She wrote:

> We don't have any children in the home, [but] my husband and I were both excited to learn and live the Savior's teachings. Scripture study became something that we looked forward to rather than another task that needed to be completed. We also had less arguments, fulfilling the promise . . . that the influence of the adversary in our home would decrease. We love how *Come, Follow Me* has changed our lives for the better.

One of the frequently overlooked benefits of engaging in gospel learning together as spouses and families is that doing so provides a common language, a shared story, a common topic of discussion.[8] This is a small means that can bring forward great things. The marital researcher John Gottman has noted that the strongest and most enduring marriages tend to involve "emotionally intelligent couples [who] are intimately familiar with each other's world."[9] When a significant part of that world is shared through gospel learning, study, interaction, and discussion, everyone wins. These efforts to be on the same page can combine with the inherent "virtue of the word of God" to yield a "powerful effect" (Alma 31:5). One such effect noted by some members was a decrease in arguments and contention, as mentioned by parents and spouses in a variety of circumstances:

> "We have had increased power to overcome challenges, have been guided as to how we could serve others, and have noticed less contention in our daily lives."

> "Our family has found hope through the *Come, Follow Me* program. The influence of the adversary in our home has decreased. We are kinder. We love deeper. Our home is brighter."

> "There has been a more peaceful feeling within our home. Others have even commented on it."

The reports mesh well with social science studies, including our own, that indicate that "shared religious involvement . . . appears to promote higher levels of marital adjustment and commitment."[10] Further, shared religious practices and beliefs (for example, *Come, Follow Me*) can help couples and families "prevent, resolve, and overcome . . . conflict and [help] in resolving conflict."[11]

We were encouraged to hear related positive reports from some part-member families as well, despite significant inherent difficulties. One person wrote that despite the challenges, she wanted others to know that "these blessings occur even in a part-member family." One husband wrote that "[*Come, Follow Me*] adds a level of peace to our home, even though we're a part-member family. Contention seems to go down, and my wife seems more willing to discuss gospel topics since I . . . bring them up more often now."

Is President Nelson's third promise being fulfilled? Is the influence of the adversary decreasing? With respect to the three prophetic promises, some individuals and families are reaping and reporting fairly dramatic changes, while others are seeing incremental progress, including a member who wrote, in summary, "I feel the three promises are slowly improving my quality of life." In most cases, the Lord works with His children in ways that allow their conversion to occur "line upon line; here a little, and there a little" (Isaiah 28:13), although others do have more dramatic conversion events.

The reports of those experiencing dramatic and gradual improvements despite increased opposition inspire us to do better and be better and to lay claim to the prophetically promised blessings. However, as we reviewed members' reports, we were reminded that our Heavenly Father frequently chooses to deliver even more than He promises. In the next chapter, we turn our attention to some "bonus blessings" (unexpected blessings) that our fellow members of the Church of Jesus Christ reported.

QUESTIONS TO ENCOURAGE CONTEMPLATION AND CONVERSATION

1. Pulitzer Prize–winning author Robert Coles has observed that great books issue a moral call to us as readers to be better people. How have you experienced and felt that call as you have studied the scriptures?

2. The Lord has urged us to diligently seek learning "out of the best books," including and especially the scriptures. How can you and your family increase your diligence in learning from the best books, including but not limited to the scriptures?

3. President Nelson has offered at least three prophetic promises to us as we seek to "remodel [our] home into a center of gospel learning." These promises, to be fulfilled "over time," are that "*your* Sabbath days will truly be a delight. *Your* children will be excited to learn and to live the Savior's teachings, and the influence of the adversary in *your* life and in *your* home will decrease." Have you seen these promises begin to be fulfilled in your personal and family life?

4. Of the blessings mentioned by the members referenced in this chapter, was there one that was especially meaningful or striking to you? If so, how can you seek a similar blessing?
5. This chapter suggests that "it is not enough to teach the Lord's doctrine. We must also strive to teach His doctrine *in the manner and spirit* that He taught it—namely, through word and example, with profound love, with a listening ear, and with respect." What are the personal implications of this principle for you?

CREATING OPPORTUNITIES FOR REVELATORY EXPERIENCES (CORE)

1. What intentions do you have to enjoy personal revelatory experiences?
2. How can you and your loved ones encourage each other's revelatory experiences?
3. What personal and relational activities might encourage your own revelatory experiences?

NOTES

1. See Robert Coles, *The Call of Stories: Teaching and the Moral Imagination* (Boston: Houghton Mifflin, 1990).
2. Joseph Smith, "History, 1838–1856, volume C-1 [2 November 1838–31 July 1842]," p. 1255, The Joseph Smith Papers, https://www.josephsmithpapers.org/paper-summary/history-1838-1856-volume-c-1-2-november-1838-31-july-1842/427.
3. Russell M. Nelson, "Becoming Exemplary Latter-day Saints," *Ensign*, November 2018, 113.
4. Nelson, "Becoming Exemplary Latter-day Saints," 113.
5. David C. Dollahite and Loren Marks, "Mormons' Weekly Family Ritual Is an Antidote to Fast-Paced Living," *Atlantic*, March 29, 2018, https://www.theatlantic.com/family/archive/2018/03/mormon-family-home-evening/556658/.
6. Heather Howell Kelley, email message, October 2020.
7. Loren Marks, quoted in Lois M. Collins, "How Parents Pass Their Religious Beliefs on to Children, Knowing They May Walk Away," *Deseret News*, January 23, 2020, https://www.deseret.com/indepth/2020/1/23/21076871/byu-faith-religion-prayer-pew-research-center-notre-dame-children-rights-david-dollahite-loren-marks.
8. See David Dollahite and Loren Marks, "'Holy Script!' Sacred Text in the Home," January 12, 2020, in *One Page at a Time*, podcast, https://onepagepodcast.com/2020/01/12/15-holy-script-sacred-text-in-the-home-with-dr-david-dollahite-and-dr-loren-marks/.
9. John M. Gottman and Nan Silver, *The Seven Principles for Making Marriage Work* (New York: Three Rivers, 2004), 48.
10. Loren D. Marks and David C. Dollahite, *Religion and Families: An Introduction* (New York: Routledge, 2017), 59.

11. Nathaniel M. Lambert and David C. Dollahite, "How Religiosity Helps Couples Prevent, Resolve, and Overcome Marital Conflict," *Family Relations* 55, no. 4 (October 2006): 439–49.

CHAPTER EIGHT

More Than Promised: Unexpected Additional Blessings

In the previous chapter, we reported what members wrote about the blessings they had received in connection with the three specific promises President Russell M. Nelson made to the Saints. As a review, these were the promises he made: "I promise that as you diligently work to remodel your home into a center of gospel learning, over time [1] *your* Sabbath days will truly be a delight. [2] *Your* children will be excited to learn and to live the Savior's teachings, and [3] the influence of the adversary in *your* life and in *your* home will decrease."[1]

Members shared an array of responses to the question regarding whether they had seen these promises fulfilled. One parent wrote, "[It] depends on the evening [and the] topic of study. Sometimes our kids participate, and sometimes they won't say a word." Yes, most parents have been there.

For other members, the answer seemed to be variations of "I have not seen these blessings fulfilled yet, but I am still trying to lay claim to them by pushing forward in faith." As one member wrote, "[I am] hoping and praying these promises will become a reality in my life. I trust in the Lord that if I am faithful and obedient, good things will happen."

Others offered hope for all of those who, like the member just quoted, are hoping that these blessings will become a reality. Many individuals and parents, mothers and fathers, did share their own version of a statement from a parent who wrote, "We have seen these promises fulfilled." Our hope is that we will all eventually share that same experience and conviction.

In our work as social scientists, we often use in-depth interviews that ask specific, careful questions because we need specific insights. However, we also tend to pay particular attention when ideas we did *not* ask about are repeatedly mentioned and discussed. We call these concepts "spontaneous themes."

Along those lines, some important blessings were mentioned spontaneously by members so frequently (in response to questions about the three promises) that these blessings demanded our attention. In this chapter, we will mention three.

The three additional blessings all dealt with increased love in relationships: (1) a closer relationship with the Savior and the Spirit, (2) deeper and more loving family relationships, and (3) closer connection with ward or branch members.

These three additional blessings seem to combine to deliver on a prophetic promise from President Nelson that great blessings will come as we "unleash the power of families."[2] This increased and integrated love of God and family also captures what President Dallin H. Oaks taught in an October 2019 general conference address: "I begin with what Jesus taught were the two great commandments. 'Thou shalt love the Lord thy God with all thy heart, and with all thy soul, and with all thy mind. This is the first and great commandment. And the second is like unto it, Thou shalt love thy neighbour as thyself' [Matthew 22:37–39]. This means we are commanded to love everyone, since Jesus's parable of the good Samaritan teaches that everyone is our neighbor."[3]

President Oaks continued and admonished Church members that "our zeal to keep this second commandment must not cause us to forget the first, to love God with all our heart, soul, and mind."[4] In our list of additional blessings, we begin with the blessing of a closer relationship with the Savior and the Spirit.

ADDITIONAL BLESSING 1: A CLOSER RELATIONSHIP WITH THE SAVIOR AND THE SPIRIT

In this vein, members who reported on the blessings of home-centered gospel study frequently mentioned an increased closeness with and love of the Savior. One member wrote of *Come, Follow Me*, "It has help[ed] me to keep my focus on the SAVIOR more." A sister without children at home wrote:

> I have found a new love for Christ. . . . I feel closer to the Lord and more aware of His life and what He would do in situations similar to mine.

Another member wrote:

> I study more as an individual and have strengthened my own testimony of the Savior this year. [It has also] strengthened my family's testimonies.

An older sister wrote:

> I've enjoyed studying the accounts of the Savior's life and experiences. I am a seasoned, long-time member with a testimony and have studied these accounts before. But this time, I have had a whole different, sweeter feeling for the Savior and have felt his love and gentleness through this study.

Next, we offer several other members' experiences relating to *Come, Follow Me* study, learning, and worship. Note that each of these members, like those just referenced, specifically mentions "the Savior," "my Savior," or "our Savior":

> "Another benefit [of *Come, Follow Me*] has been an increase of patience with each other as we navigate our busy lives. Thinking of the Savior and His teachings daily has brought gratitude and helped us to strive to become like Him."
>
> "I study alone, but using the [*Come, Follow Me*] study guide and sincerely asking myself the questions has increased my love for the Savior [even] more than . . . teaching seminary and institute."
>
> "We have become closer to our Savior and each other."
>
> "I have felt a distinct shift in my ability to address and work through some difficult circumstances in my life. I have been able to more clearly comprehend the direction my Savior would have me take."

Another member wrote the following as encouragement:

> The purpose of *Come, Follow Me* is to draw closer to our Savior, Jesus Christ. If you get behind, don't stress out, and don't feel guilty. Just ask Heavenly Father for help, study a little bit every day, and I promise you will receive that blessing of drawing closer to Christ.

In addition to many references to the Savior, some members also mentioned an increased sensitivity to the Spirit. One member wrote that *Come, Follow Me* "has helped me grow personally and feel the Spirit confirming the truth of the messages." Another reported that in addition to the promised prophetic blessings, "my ability to discern . . . the promptings and guidance of [the] Holy Ghost has definitely increased. . . . I am so thankful for prophetic promises and a Savior who truly loves me!"

One individual wrote, "[My] spiritual awareness has increased greatly." Another observed:

> Since I have been devoting attention to *Come, Follow Me* lessons, related scriptural readings, and discussions at home, I have noticed that I have been receiving more spiritual impressions about a variety of things.

Another parent wrote that in addition to other blessings,

> I also feel the Spirit more in our home as we read together. It helps us discuss the scriptures instead of just read them.

One memorable and encouraging testimony referenced both the Spirit and the Savior. Like many members who shared their reports and reflections, this individual had experienced the three prophetically promised blessings but was not content to note only those three blessings, adding,

> Another thing for me personally: I have felt the promptings from the Spirit more in my life. I have faced things this past year that I have been running from for years. I can only attribute that strength to the strength of the Savior—because it hasn't been easy, but I have had the courage to be stronger and to face my fears. I feel an urge to study more and to feast, as Nephi says, on the words [of Christ]. I am learning so much more than I have ever learned [before]. It's exciting that all of this happened in just a year! I am excited for the changes in my life!

It was encouraging to hear members' reports of closer connections with the Savior and the Spirit. However, if deeper relationships with the Lord are where the additional reported blessings began, it is not where they ended. Many members addressed improvements in their family relationships as well.

ADDITIONAL BLESSING 2: DEEPER AND MORE LOVING FAMILY RELATIONSHIPS

Many members reported that engaging in home-centered study of the gospel had influenced and motivated positive changes in their marital and family relationships. One parent and grandparent wrote:

> Our family has grown closer as we have studied the scriptures together. We had a granddaughter living with us for a while, and *Come, Follow Me* study with her helped us know her better and increased our love for her and for each other.

One wife reported extraordinary dedication on the part of herself and her husband:

> My husband and I have followed [*Come, Follow Me*] every night for a year. We don't have children at home, but [as we study] we get different ideas of how to serve our less active children. It has been a blessing to us each night as we study in bed; [studying has brought] a real sense of peace.

Another wife and mother wrote:

> We have all improved in different aspects of our li[ves]. My husband is not only a better father but a better husband and is even excelling in the workplace. I have also made strides to make a happier and [more] positive home.

One member wrote of her marriage:

> Our relationship . . . is deeper as we talk about the Master more in our daily conversations. It's becoming the norm, and we feel "lighter" in the burdens we have been carrying.

One husband explained that *Come, Follow Me* has been the catalyst for other efforts in his shared gospel living efforts with his wife:

> My wife is a convert and the only member [in] her family, so [*Come, Follow Me*] has been a natural point of focus for us as a family, both last year and this year. Our weekly temple attendance as a family has been very rewarding, doing the work for my wife's family. [All of] this has been greatly spurred on by the Sunday family gospel study and the deep feelings it inspires in us.

We shift from the relational and spiritual blessings associated with shared family learning and worship and touch briefly on an important social science finding. In a previous chapter, we discussed the decades-long marital research of psychologist John Gottman and his discovery that one vital factor that creates thriving, loving, and vibrant marriages is the ability of couples to be "intimately familiar with each other's world."[5] How is this done? What is the secret? Gottman gives us the following: "We wondered what would distinguish those couples whose marriages continued to improve from those whose marriages did not. . . . We discovered that [successful couples] were devoting . . . an extra five hours a week to their marriage. . . . I've come to call it the Magic Five Hours."[6]

For Gottman, those "Magic Five Hours" should consist of a weekly two-hour date and then an ideal total of thirty minutes a day to share meaningful time. Along with home evening[7] and other home-centered religious practices, could *Come, Follow Me* be a core part of those Magic Five Hours? An older married couple wrote that as they have been studying, learning, and discussing together, they have been "growing closer to each other and our Savior TOGETHER."

An additional leading marriage expert, William J. Doherty, shared a similar message about shared time together. He wrote, "If a married couple with children has fifteen minutes of uninterrupted, nonproblem-solving talk every day, I would put them in the top five percent of all married couples in the land. It's an extraordinary achievement. . . . [However], mumbling at 11 o'clock at night when you are exhausted does not count."[8]

Does *Come, Follow Me* "count"? Does couple prayer count? Do temple visits count? If couples engage in such activities with attentive love, patience, and kindness, then yes. The inspired structure of the gospel generally (and perhaps the *Come, Follow Me* invitation specifically) can help provide these "Magic Hours" and minutes that can not only preserve our marriages and families but increasingly strengthen them.

Let's take a brief look at single phrases from members' *Come, Follow Me* reports that we consider anew:

"Our family has grown closer as we have studied the scriptures together."

"*Come, Follow Me* study [has] increased our love . . . for each other."

"It has been a blessing to us each night as we study."

> "Our relationship . . . is deeper as we talk about the Master more."

> "[We are grateful for] family gospel study and the deep feelings it inspires in us."

The reports above and others like them yield a hope that dedicated efforts to *Come, Follow Me* not only bring individuals closer to the Savior and the Spirit—these efforts also often seem to help strengthen marriages and families.

ADDITIONAL BLESSING 3: CLOSER CONNECTION WITH WARD OR BRANCH MEMBERS

However, what about our single, widowed, or divorced sisters and brothers who now make up a majority of adult Church members?[9] In the previous chapter, we heard from some who felt their single status was painfully underscored by the emphasis on family study—and we urged member families to consider ways to involve singles in mutually beneficial ways.

Gratefully, however, there were also many encouraging reports from single members that highlighted blessings received and perceived as a result of efforts to engage in *Come, Follow Me*. These blessings included a closer sense of connection with extended family and with ward or branch members.

One member who is single discussed all three of the additional blessings outlined in this chapter by referencing how deeper gospel studying, learning, and worship have connected her more closely with "the Savior, [her] family, and ward members." She explained:

> Living alone, I can also testify that I feel more connected to the Savior, my family, and ward members, because I know they are striving for the same goal [to engage in more meaningful study and worship]. This feeling of connection makes me feel strengthened against the influence of the adversary. Studying has also deepened my relationship with the Savior, and even though trials [and] temptations have not been

removed, because of my deeper relationship with Him I feel more fortified and confident in withstanding [and] overcoming them.

Another single member wrote:

> I am not married and do not have children, [but] I do feel power in my life and home from the Lord, and [I] enjoy Sabbath day study and journal time. I feel the Lord is guiding, directing, and comforting me in my life. The power in the lives of the children in my life, at church, and in my [extended] family seems to be increasing for good.

We think it is significant that both of these members note beneficial impacts and blessings at church. For some (and perhaps many) members, the unified and coordinated *Come, Follow Me* invitation helps foster unity—not only by drawing those who follow the invitation closer to the Lord but also by drawing single sisters and brothers closer to those in their ward who are on the same page (or at least are in the same few chapters).

One BYU student, a returned sister missionary who is single, wrote the following about her own personal study and worship:

> One day as I studied the scriptures, I sought teaching from the Lord about the topic of love. His divine lesson surprised me. He told me that I have the tendency to focus on others but that He wants me to focus on Him. [The message I received was] "As you strengthen your relationship with me, then your relationships with others will naturally become more strengthened as well. Focus on loving me."
>
> The depth and quality of your relationship with Him will translate to your relationships with others. So the question becomes "How can I strengthen my relationship with Thee?" President Oaks gives us one suggestion: "We show that love by 'keep[ing] His commandments.'"[10] By living His commandments and keeping our covenants, we draw nearer to Christ.
>
> One day my roommates and I talked about our "love languages," which brought me to ponder, "What's Christ's love language? How

does He feel loved?" When we live our covenants and keep His commandments, He feels loved. Our covenants are Christ's love language. By living our covenants, we draw nearer to Christ. (John 14:15—"If ye love me, keep my commandments.")

The message of this woman and many other diverse members who reported on their *Come, Follow Me* efforts was that devoted personal and family study and worship can intensify our love for Christ and bring an increased focus on Him and our Father. Our heightened love of the Savior and our Father then blesses all other relationships, helping us to be nobler children in the family of God.

In summary, in addition to the prophetic promises of home-centered gospel learning yielding "Sabbath days [that] will truly be a delight," "children [that] will be excited to learn and to live the Savior's teachings," and a decreasing "influence of the adversary in [our] li[ves] and in [our] home[s],"[11] there were significant additional blessings that members repeatedly mentioned. These blessings included a closer relationship with the Savior and the Spirit. Reported blessings also included an additional closeness between wife and husband, parent and child, and grandparent and grandchild. Some mentioned that these blessings even seemed to stretch into relationships with adult children and children who were not actively walking the covenant path.

Finally, for some, including for several single members, the additional relational blessings were not constrained to family but spilled over into feelings of increased unity, closeness, and connection with ward or branch members.

President Nelson has encouraged the Saints to draw closer to the Lord, to hear Him, to feast on the word of God, and to remain on the covenant path. In so doing he has offered prophetic blessings and promises to those who follow this counsel. He has taught:

> Our Father loves us and yearns for each one of us to *choose* to return to His holy presence. He pleads with us to listen to the voice of Jesus Christ, whom the Father anointed and appointed as our Mediator, Savior, and Redeemer.

> . . . I invite you to think deeply and often about this key question: How do *you* hear Him? I also invite you to take steps to hear Him better and more often. . . .
>
> Now, as one of the Lord's special witnesses, I bless you in your efforts to get on and stay on His covenant path, and strive with all your heart, might, mind and soul to *Hear Him!*[12]

In an additional message, he said:

> Brothers and sisters, I thank you for your faith and sustaining efforts. I leave my love and blessing upon you, that you may feast upon the word of the Lord and apply His teachings in your personal lives. I assure you that revelation continues in the Church and will continue until "the purposes of God shall be accomplished, and the Great Jehovah shall say the work is done" [*Teachings of Presidents of the Church: Joseph Smith* (2007), 142].[13]

The Lord's prophet then concluded by stating yet another series of blessings that we can receive if we are willing:

> I bless you with increased faith in Him and in His holy work, with faith and patience to endure your personal challenges in life. I bless you to become exemplary Latter-day Saints. I so bless you and bear my testimony that God lives! Jesus is the Christ! This is His Church. We are His people, in the name of Jesus Christ, amen.[14]

QUESTIONS TO ENCOURAGE CONTEMPLATION AND CONVERSATION

1. President Oaks has reminded Church members that "our zeal to keep th[e] second commandment must not cause us to forget the first, to love God with all our heart, soul, and mind." What meaning do you draw from this reminder?

2. This chapter focuses on additional blessings beyond those that have been promised. Have there been times in your life when you have felt blessed for your obedience in even more ways than promised?

3. Have you felt deeper connection with your Heavenly Father, your Savior, and the Spirit as you have engaged in personal study and worship?
4. Have you felt deeper connection with family members as you have engaged in family study and worship?
5. Have you felt deeper connection with other ward members as you have responded to the invitation to "come, follow me"?
6. What are the implications of the "Magic Five Hours" for you and your relationships?

CREATING OPPORTUNITIES FOR REVELATORY EXPERIENCES (CORE)

1. What intentions do you have to enjoy personal revelatory experiences?
2. How can you and your loved ones encourage each other's revelatory experiences?
3. What personal and relational activities might encourage your own revelatory experiences?

NOTES

1. Russell M. Nelson, "Becoming Exemplary Latter-day Saints," *Ensign*, November 2018, 113.
2. Nelson, "Becoming Exemplary Latter-day Saints," 113.
3. Dallin H. Oaks, "*Two* Great Commandments," *Ensign*, November 2019, 73.
4. Oaks, "*Two* Great Commandments," 73–74.
5. John M. Gottman and Nan Silver, *The Seven Principles for Making Marriage Work* (New York: Three Rivers, 2004), 48.
6. Gottman and Silver, *Seven Principles*, 260.
7. See Loren D. Marks et al., "The Real Book of Mormon Musical: Latter-day Saint Family Home Evening as a Weekly Ritual," *Marriage & Family Review* 56, no. 5 (2020): 425–48.
8. William J. Doherty, *Take Back Your Marriage: Sticking Together in a World That Pulls Us Apart* (New York: Guilford, 2013), 130.
9. See Gerrit W. Gong, "Room in the Inn," *Ensign*, May 2021, 26.
10. Oaks, "*Two* Great Commandments," 74.
11. Nelson, "Becoming Exemplary Latter-day Saints," 113.
12. Russell M. Nelson, "'How Do You #HearHim?' A Special Invitation," February 26, 2020, ChurchofJesusChrist.org; emphasis in original.
13. Nelson, "Becoming Exemplary Latter-day Saints," 114.
14. Nelson, "Becoming Exemplary Latter-day Saints," 114.

CHAPTER NINE

Envisioning Home-Centered Religious Life after a Global Pandemic

This chapter contains ideas about moving forward with home-centered religious life in the shadow of the COVID-19 pandemic. We provide some findings from research we did in 2020 about how individuals, couples, and families adjusted toward more home-centered religious life because of the shutdowns resulting from the pandemic. We hope the ideas and participant quotes herein will give you food for thought as you and your loved ones move forward.

We strive to be what Elder Neal A. Maxwell called "disciple-scholars"[1] and treasure both our membership in the Church of Jesus Christ (and all the gospel entails) and our opportunity to study family and faith using the tools of the social sciences. With both realities noted, we value our religious identity far more than our scholarly identity. We strive to be disciples of Jesus Christ before, while, and after we are family scholars. We have been blessed to have a largely shared professional career that has allowed us to study the principles and processes upon which strong and faithful families are founded. We are grateful that our work at BYU has allowed us to spend our days learning and teaching about both prophetic teachings and social science research regarding how to build happy and successful marriages and families.

In his book *The Spirit of Revelation*, David A. Bednar emphasized that revelation is "scattered among us" and that as we listen to one another we can learn important truths regarding how the Spirit has worked with our sisters and brothers in God's family.[2] We have been blessed to listen to, read, and analyze the spoken and written words (more than two million of them) of many hundreds of people of faith from various religious communities,[3] and we have learned much from them. As we have carefully studied the ways that God has worked with and through good people from many diverse racial and religious backgrounds, we have been enriched. We hope that it has been a blessing for you to have read the words of fellow Saints and of inspiring friends from other faiths.

PRESCIENT PROPHETS AND POST-PANDEMIC PROGRESS

Whatever the long-term effects of COVID-19 in our society, President Nelson's prophetic vision for moving toward a home-centered, Church-supported approach to gospel learning has been shown to be prescient. The *Come, Follow Me* initiative was presented to the Church in October 2018, more than a year before the various shutdowns—including those associated with religious gatherings—were in place. These home-centered changes served as a preparation for and protection against some of the challenges of COVID, including dramatic changes such as the extended closure of community faith worship and the loss of support many draw from sacred gatherings spiritually, emotionally, socially, and relationally. It is certain that we have entered a period in Church history in which home-centered religious life and the need for personal and interpersonal revelatory experiences will be as important as—if not more important than—any prior time in world or Church history.

FAMILY RESPONSES TO THE COVID-19 PANDEMIC

In an essay on family relationships during COVID-19, family psychologist Jay Lebow quoted Dickens's famous opening line from *A Tale of Two Cities*, "It was the best of times, it was the worst of times," as he discussed the "intense period for family life" experienced on a global scale that made for "powerful shared processes."[4] During and after the pandemic, we were deeply interested to learn how families, especially religious families, were navigating their faith life and practices. With generous support from the Wheatley Institution and BYU's School of Family Life, we surveyed a diverse array of 1,510 people around the United States to gather insight regarding what families from a variety of faiths, races, and regions were finding helpful.

We have subsequently published five scholarly articles[5] on five different family-related aspects of COVID. These include (1) family financial stress, (2) spiritual practices, (3) religious practices, (4) family communication, and (5) shared family meals. At thirty-five pages each, the articles would (and may) comprise an additional book, but in this chapter, we share a few high points and key findings that shed additional light on home-based worship and family relationships, drawn from the latter three articles: the articles on religious practices, family communication, and shared family meals.

RELIGIOUS PRACTICES DURING COVID-19

Families from a variety of faiths shared much with us regarding religious practices, including and especially family prayer, scripture study, shared sacred rituals, and home-based worship. Perhaps the most striking single finding from our COVID-19 survey of religious families in the United States was that 60 percent of people reported that because of their increased engagement in religious practices in their homes during the pandemic, they believed these changes would have a lasting positive effect on their family. One Protestant parent said:

> [During COVID] we started praying together at meals more consistently.... This is a practice that has given us comfort and peace during these unpredictable times. I believe that we will continue to pray together more often as we move forward.

Another Protestant parent said:

> [After COVID-19 hit,] we learned how to make better use of our time to make more time for our faith. We learned that it was not that we did not have enough time to read the Bible [and do] devotions. . . . It was that we were spending our time on the wrong things. This [change] will have a lasting positive influence in our lives, because our lives . . . have been much more positive.

In addition to family prayer and scripture study, several participants explained that they found meaning and strength in sacred rituals. Some members of The Church of Jesus Christ of Latter-day Saints mentioned ordinances. One mother reported the following about her eight-year-old daughter's baptism:

> Our middle child was baptized during the [COVID] shutdown. It was an amazing spiritual experience, since only us and our bishop were in attendance. We did a Zoom call with family members, but there were just us five and the bishop. Instead of worrying [about] who would be there, who would bring what to the luncheon, where we would hold the luncheon, what we would eat, . . . our focus was on the ordinance itself. I think it made it so much more meaningful. . . . I've never been so focused on an ordinance . . . before.

Continuing the theme of sacred ordinances and rituals, one Jewish parent reported that

> this year we made a point of participating in a Passover seder via Zoom with the extended family. It felt right and important to do this at this questionable time of human existence. We also are planning to stay in the area through the fall, because there will be a family bat mitzvah in October and a bar mitzvah in December. . . . In a time of questioning our life span and possible mortality, it definitely seems more important to be at family events and life-cycle events such as these.

Sacred rituals were frequently changed as a result of the COVID-19 shutdown but still retained their meaning—and in many cases the meaning and sacred nature were deepened.

Similarly, during the COVID shutdown many families replaced their faith community worship with additional home-based worship. One Muslim parent said:

> My view of the importance of home-centered worship has made every aspect of my relationship better because we were able to connect to God and each other in a positive way. We were able to work out our differences as well.

A mother from the Church of Jesus Christ said:

> [Before COVID hit,] we weren't very good at doing the home-centered church study . . . but with COVID we began doing it weekly, because if we didn't, we wouldn't receive any type of religious practice within our home. My husband has also been recently struggling with his faith, and . . . COVID . . . has helped recenter him. He is using his [faith] in the home and seeing how important it is. It hasn't solved all of our faith-based struggles, but it has helped.

Pauline Boss, a leading researcher of family stress, has noted that a crisis is an opportunity to rise up and do better and be more than we were before the event hit us.[6] Some families accepted that opportunity as an invitation.

Family prayer, scripture study, sacred rituals, and home-based worship are four powerful religious practices that our participants repeatedly referenced, but there is another home-based practice that may be the most influential of all—sharing family meals.

SHARED FAMILY MEALS DURING COVID-19

A wealth of previous social science research has identified the connections between regular family dinners and stronger parent-child relationships and improved child outcomes.[7] Family dinners seem to be especially positive for adolescents, with benefits ranging from buffering against family conflict[8] to promoting healthier eating habits and lowering risk of obesity[9] to reducing the incidence of risk-taking behaviors.[10] Further, the leading scholar on shared family meals, Professor Barbara Fiese, has also documented the power of family routines and rituals to benefit adults and children during times of stress and change. This reality seems to indicate that shared meals are an especially important concern during the COVID era.[11]

In our survey research with hundreds of diverse American parents, we found that families that reported engaging in regular family dinner reported significantly higher levels of family emotional closeness[12] than those who did not. We gained several additional insights from 130 open-ended comments from parents addressing shared family meals, including the three recurring themes discussed below.

First, many parents reported that COVID stimulated an *increase* in shared family meals. One said, "We enjoyed having dinner together every night. Normally, we would be rushing to make it to practices or getting home late from practice and games, so dinner was rushed and we got to spend very little time together. Since COVID-19 [closures], we have had more quality time spen[t] together."

Some readers might question why we are spending time addressing shared family meals in a book that is focused on home-centered religious life and sharing revelatory experiences. In our research on families during COVID, we learned that for many parents and families, *family meals and family prayers were a package deal*. We were struck by the frequency of combined references to the two practices. However, there was something else that captured our attention. In the following "prayer at dinner" reports from a diverse array of parents, we use italics to draw special attention to the centrality of the first-person plural pronoun "we" and the accompanying *together*ness that participants conveyed as they discussed family coping during COVID.

"*We* pray over meals and with our kids each night."

"*We* as a family stayed *together* during this time. *We* eat *together*. *We* are doing prayer *together*. This is giving strength to [the] entire family [to] cope with any fear."

"[To cope], *we* . . . spend more time *together* [and] eat *together* and pray *together*."

"*We* normalize praying *together*, eating [*together*,] and having exercise [*together*,] and this really helped us. Also, praying helped us with our mental and emotional health. *We* get to free our minds and share bothering things."

"*We* talk a lot at dinner, and *we* call things to our blessing and prayers."

"[To help us get through], *we* . . . eat dinner as a family and pray [*together*]. I think having dinner *together* strengthen[s] our relationship."

Most of the above comments (from Catholic, Protestant, Latter-day Saint, and religiously unaffiliated parents) were stimulated by a question related to family coping. Several other "prayer at dinner" responses came from participants who reported changes in family practices that were stimulated by COVID:

"[Since COVID hit, we do] more family prayers at the dinner table and at bedtime."

"[Since COVID,] we pray more at the dinner table."

"[The pandemic] made us all [stop and get] together, praying almost on each meal. We are together hoping that [God] will lift this pandemic and make us peaceful."

Another related report came from a Protestant parent who responded, "A lasting positive way [we have changed from COVID] is more regular prayer with each other. [We now pray] at mealtimes, in the morning, and also before bed. . . . And that will be a lasting positive effect."

For another parent, a Catholic, a shift to increased home-centered worship was not only hoped for but realized—and "graces before meals" served as an important context for familial and religious unity. The parent reported:

> The lasting positive effects of the COVID-19 shutdown [are] that my children see that [we] continue to practice our religious practices such as hearing Mass on Sundays as well as saying the rosary and graces before meals. . . . The COVID-19 shutdown made our family closer, since we are together more often. It has reinforced the practice of turning to God and to religion when there is fear and uncertainty, especially when there are things that we cannot solve by ourselves.

To this point, we have summarized key findings from our recent social science articles on religious practices and shared family meals. As we now turn to the third and final topic, family communication, we will summarize the related article's findings that address important considerations for families and home-centered worship during the COVID era.

FAMILY COMMUNICATION DURING COVID-19

Of our 1,510 US survey participants in the COVID study, 624 also chose to respond to some open-ended questions. One participant captured an encouraging change:

> [COVID] offered us the opportunity to connect more often with relatives living farther away who were feeling socially isolated without their peer groups. We established a new normal for communicating with loved ones more frequently.

Indeed, in the open-ended responses, there were repeated mentions of what we call "the Zoom boom" that spanned through generations and extended families. Next, we list three excerpts from 142 Zoom-related reports:

> "I have been on Zoom together with several of my cousins that I have not been in touch with for over ten years."

> "We . . . focused on building relationships with our kids/grandkids/relatives who live out of state by setting weekly Zoom calls where we all got together and shared. We also had family Zoom dance parties. . . .

[All of this] has actually built our relationships, as everyone had more time to be together that way."

"One thing that my family did was . . . do family game nights over Zoom to stay in contact with one another and to not be so lonely. This made all of us happier and . . . feel close to one another, even though we live in different states. This was something different to do and really helped deal with the stress of quarantine."

Again, some may wonder what families connecting through Zoom might have to do with this book's theme of building eternal families through home-centered worship and revelatory experiences. Consider the next two responses, which both indicate that the respondents' family Zoom gatherings occurred on the Sabbath. One person said, "[Our family] began having Zoom Sundays where we shared our thoughts and frustrations with each other." Another reported, "I have nine brothers and sisters. Just about every week we Zoom together on Sunday evenings. We did not do this before COVID-19." Such reports are not limited to participants in our research; we have had some significant personal experiences that we share later in this chapter.

TAKEAWAYS FROM OUR COVID-19 STUDIES

The effects of the pandemic include economic, financial, political, educational, occupational, cultural, religious, and relational changes, stresses, and losses. The nature of these effects, including the effects of religious-service shutdowns, range from devastatingly negative to surprisingly positive. As many members of The Church of Jesus Christ of Latter-day Saints have dealt with the many changes and challenges brought by the pandemic, they have felt blessed by (a) the "head start" on home-centered worship and study provided by the 2018–19 announcements and implementation of *Come, Follow Me*, (b) the lay nature of the priesthood that allowed many to receive the sacrament in their own homes, and (c) the ongoing guidance and comfort provided by living prophets, seers, and revelators.

The opportunity to spend more time at home with family members, the opportunity to practice the skills learned and patterns established from the *Come, Follow Me* curriculum, and the increased sense of gratitude for a living prophet have likely strengthened the faith of many Saints, even as they are aware that others—including some loved ones and dear friends—are experiencing increasing doubts around religious beliefs and involvement.

The fact that the pandemic seems to have encouraged more attention to family meals is an encouraging counter to the trend toward less regular family meals that has existed for decades. The additional fact that, for many families, regular prayer is deeply associated with regular meals is another positive by-product of the pandemic. And if the pandemic Zoom boom has allowed and encouraged more families to connect with one another across distances—including for religious reasons—then that too is something to celebrate.

GLOBAL PANDEMICS AND GROWTH POSSIBILITIES

During 2020–22 (and likely beyond), the world faced the COVID-19 global pandemic that has infected hundreds of millions, killed more than six million, and significantly affected almost everyone's life.[13] Given all the challenges and fears associated with the pandemic, it is typical to think of the negative effects: loss of life, decreased personal security, increased unemployment, loss of income, threats to businesses and livelihoods, and major disruptions in personal and family routines.

A crisis, however, is also an opportunity for growth. The existential crisis that any one of us could be infected with a life-threatening illness has led many people to question certain aspects of their lives, such as their priorities, schedules, and relationships. Indeed, the pandemic has also been an invitation for individuals, couples, and families to reconsider what is most meaningful, essential, and important. Because of the societal shutdowns and increased time spent at home, away from their normal routines and responsibilities, many also have envisioned or reenvisioned what they desire for their personal, spiritual, marital, and family lives. COVID-19 has allowed people to reprioritize their lives in ways that give greater importance to home life and relationships. We hope and pray that once life fully returns to normal—or more likely to a "new normal"—we will not lapse back into old patterns that place faith and family somewhere other than priority number one.

In an April 2020 *Church News* article about the COVID-19 crisis, Elder Quentin L. Cook placed the *Come, Follow Me* initiative and the home-centered, Church-supported approach in a broader context of revelation about several other issues. He said, "Each of us, in our current circumstances, can have a home that is a sanctuary of faith," and he offered the hope that "we will look back on [the COVID crisis] as a foundational time of preparation, and not just something we had to endure." Elder Cook also said:

> Perhaps recent events can be a spiritual alarm clock focusing us on those things that matter most. If so, it will be a great blessing in this period to concentrate on things that we can perfect in our lives and how we can bless the lives of others as we awaken to God and move along the covenant path.[14]

Elder Cook's encouragement "to concentrate on things that we can perfect in our lives" and then to consider "how we can bless the lives of others as we awaken to God and move along the covenant path" bears remarkable similarity to Jesus's aforementioned charge to Peter: "I have prayed for thee, that thy faith fail not: and when thou art converted, strengthen thy brethren" (Luke 22:32). Personal revelation is a personal blessing, but when our commitment to the Savior and the covenant path deepens, interpersonal revelation—revelation about "how we can bless the lives of others"—opens blessings to many souls beyond our own.

EFFECTS OF HOME-CENTERED GOSPEL LIVING

Members of The Church of Jesus Christ of Latter-day Saints are an interesting group to consider in terms of their collective responses to crises and the associated economic, social, recreational, and religious shutdowns. Because of the lay ministry and the precedent of generations of home- and family-centered religious practice, it is probably easier for Latter-day Saint families to hold religious gatherings comfortably and confidently at home than it is for many of our friends of other faiths (excepting our Jewish friends, who perhaps have an even more home-centered religion). The abundance of available blessings that flow through priesthood and prophets should elicit our profound gratitude.

Thankfully, many Latter-day Saints were authorized by Church leaders to receive the sacrament at home from a family member or ministering brother. Indeed, the number of administrations of the sacrament throughout the world during the COVID-19 shutdowns far exceeded the previous high. To contextualize, there are currently about 31,315 Latter-day Saint wards and branches globally.[15] During COVID-19 restrictions, it is probable that far more than 31,315 weekly administrations of the sacrament and related home-centered worship took place in Salt Lake City alone. Again, how grateful we should be for the literal blessings to which we have immediate access. What an opportunity to jump-start, deepen, and emphasize a home-centered approach to gospel living and learning that was introduced over a year before the pandemic.

Latter-day Saints experienced the same kinds of disruptions, challenges, and concerns as those around them, but hopefully many faithful Latter-day Saints were prepared with additional resources and were willing to share those resources with others. After all, ancient and modern prophets have taught that the last days would involve a number of major challenges, such as widespread wickedness and unbelief, societal upheavals, natural disasters, wars and rumors of wars, and a desolating scourge (see Doctrine and Covenants 5:19; 45:19–42; 88:89–91). Again, crises provide significant challenges as well as opportunities to refocus—and to serve others.

Prophets have also taught that in the last days the Lord will continually restore precious truths, gather scattered Israel, pour out the Spirit of revelation, cause His people to stand in holy places, and prepare a people to welcome the Savior when He returns to reign as Lord of Lords.

In times of significant changes and challenges, the path to joy and peace lies in profound personal conversion to Christ and His gospel and in continual revelatory experiences in communion with Heavenly Father through the Holy Spirit. These sanctifying processes can be facilitated by home-centered gospel learning and living. Home-centered religious life and meaningful revelatory experiences can be encouraged and supported by healthy family relationships and regular, meaningful family religious practices such as family prayer, scripture study, and home evening.

The Father's work and glory are to build eternal families through Christ (see Moses 1:39). Home and family worship are vital. Personal and interpersonal revelatory experiences illuminate our walk with others along the covenant path. Even so, worship and revelation are the pathway, not the ultimate destination. Our destination and eternal destiny are to be with our heavenly parents and emulate the family life that they have.

OUR EXPERIENCES WITH AND REFLECTIONS ON "HOME CHURCH"

As we mentioned in chapter 1, our own families, like all families, have imperfections, challenges, foibles, dysfunctions, and disappointments. We are all sinners. Walking toward the light is the goal. As we do so, our own sins and imperfections become illuminated and are clearer to us. We increasingly realize our need for our loving Father, for our Savior, and for eternal family support.

We profoundly appreciate the insights, experiences, and ideas we have heard from our fellow Saints who completed the *Come, Follow Me* surveys without any reward for doing so. We are impressed with their efforts, their honesty, and their optimism. Based on our experience in reading what they wrote, we believe the families who taught us would be quick to say that they are not perfect and should not be held up as paragons of *Come, Follow Me* worship. Neither are we, but here is a peek behind the doors of our homes anyway.

DAVE'S FAMILY EXPERIENCE

When our children were at home, we strove to have daily family prayer, daily scripture reading (at the dinner table between dinner and dessert), and weekly home evening. We were not perfect but were quite consistent and believe our family members and family relationships were blessed because of these religious gatherings. My wife, Mary, and I were empty nesters when President Nelson presented the *Come, Follow Me* invitation. To follow the invitation, we have both been reading the scriptures on our own and then, periodically, have spent some time together reading (or listening to) the scriptures, watching religious videos, and discussing what we read and watched, particularly on Sundays.

We loved having home church and family sacrament for the months when our ward did not meet together. We enjoyed gathering as an extended family to sing hymns, pray, read and discuss scriptures, watch Book of Mormon videos, and, especially, receive the sacrament (which one of our sons blessed and one of our grandsons passed). We loved having our oldest daughter, her husband, and their four children with us for those months and enjoyed an expanded home church experience with them. For us, there was good that resulted from the trial.

LOREN'S FAMILY EXPERIENCE

Earlier in the book, I shared my frustrated version of the "I Have a Dream" speech that included a vision in which, one blessed day, all five of my children willingly, eagerly, and unitedly would come to family scripture study and prayer the first time they were called. Alas, that misty-eyed vision has not yet become a reality.

Maybe there is a better vision, though, and COVID has provided a peek into much loftier possibilities than my "cranky dad" self sometimes sees. Two of our young single adult–aged children were sensitive to those in their circle that might benefit from joining us for *Come, Follow Me* in person—and those guests brought added light to the experience. Has everyone in our family been arriving on time? No. Have all the kids (or adults) been cheery at the outset? An even stronger "no." Were pretty dresses and dress flats sometimes juxtaposed with pajama bottoms and fuzzy slippers? Yes. But it has still been its own kind of beautiful.

There has been another blessing, a more profound one. My wife's mother, Maryann, an adult convert to The Church of Jesus Christ of Latter-day Saints, had not consistently attended Sunday worship services for many, many years before the COVID-19 pandemic. Even so, my wife, Sandra, her mother, Maryann, and our children presented me with the request to do "home church" over Zoom with Great-Grandma and Great-Grandpa, who were seven hundred miles away. As the weeks and months went by, we prayed and aimed for home church meetings that focused repeatedly on testimony and core doctrines. Our home church was dialogue rich and included both implicit and direct invitations to Great-Grandma and Great-Grandpa and to Maryann to share their insights and experiences, including Great-Grandma's conversion story. As these experiences were shared, dormant coals seemed to be coaxed again into a fire of faith. With Great-Grandpa's passing in November 2021, those four-generation family services are something we will cherish, but not only because of the memories expressed and the Spirit that was present. You see, once COVID-19 restrictions lightened and ward services resumed, Maryann returned to "ward church." However, she did not return to church alone. She brought her adult daughter Nicole with her (again and again). The day before Great-Grandpa Howald's memorial, I was able to step into the baptismal font with my wife's dear sister Nicole. Nicole's husband, Chris, one of my dearest friends, chose to be baptized three months later, and they are now preparing for the temple together. This sacred series of events can be traced to a loving request from a family member or two to do home church and *Come, Follow Me* over Zoom with extended family.

Now, when this sometimes-cranky dad reflects back on the fact that all his children got to hear their great-grandfather share his conversion from a drinking sailor to a "dry bishop" and offer his burning testimony that not even dementia could steal—and when I think that my children got to hear how their mother attended church on her own for nine years before she could be baptized at eighteen—and when I think of how one of the kids pointed out that in some ways, Great-Grandpa and Mom are faithful like Abinadi was, well, then even this cranky dad has to admit that this reality of multigenerational sharing of faith was better than my original dream of militant obedience. To paraphrase a New Testament question, "Can anything good come out of corona?" Our family might well respond, "Yes, good has come."

CONCLUSIONS REGARDING THE COVID-19 PANDEMIC AND FAMILIES

At the outset of this chapter, we stated that perhaps the most striking finding from our related studies was that 60 percent of people we interviewed reported that because of their increased engagement in religious practices in their homes during the pandemic, they believed these changes would have a lasting positive effect on their family. We shared several positive influences our participants reported, including increases in quantity and quality of family prayers, family religious activities, family meals, and family communication—and participants' hopes that they could hold on to, retain, and continue to benefit from their reprioritization of God and family as preeminent.

Our families, like many, were infected with COVID and suffered the short- and long-term symptoms but gratefully did not lose any family members to death. It is not our intent to in any way minimize the pain, suffering, and loss experienced by so many during the life-altering pandemic. Even so, based on the reports of scores of families (including our own), many learned precious lessons about the strength available through home- and family-centered worship. The blessing of the prophet Lehi to his son Jacob during their "days of . . . tribulation in the wilderness" seems applicable:

> Thou hast suffered afflictions and much sorrow. . . .
> Nevertheless, Jacob, my firstborn in the wilderness, thou knowest the greatness of God; and he shall consecrate thine afflictions for thy gain. (2 Nephi 2:1–2)

More than two years into the tribulation of COVID, it is our prayer that as you and your family remember the greatness of God and draw nearer unto Him, your afflictions will be consecrated for your gain.

QUESTIONS TO ENCOURAGE CONTEMPLATION AND CONVERSATION

1. As you reflect on your own home-centered gospel learning during the pandemic, what do you think the pandemic has taught you and your family?
2. What have you learned during the pandemic that you would want to *keep* as the world and the Church return to "normal"?

CREATING OPPORTUNITIES FOR REVELATORY EXPERIENCES (CORE)

1. What intentions do you have to enjoy personal revelatory experiences?
2. How can you and your loved ones encourage each other's revelatory experiences?
3. What personal and relational activities might encourage your own revelatory experiences?

NOTES

1. See Neal A. Maxwell, "The Disciple-Scholar," in *On Becoming a Disciple-Scholar*, ed. Henry B. Eyring (Salt Lake City: Bookcraft, 1995), 7.
2. David A. Bednar, *The Spirit of Revelation* (Salt Lake City: Deseret Book, 2021), 57–60.
3. This includes nearly seven hundred people in our American Families of Faith database, the five hundred Latter-day Saints we surveyed, and more than six hundred Americans who shared open-ended responses to our COVID-19 survey in 2020.
4. Jay L. Lebow, "Family in the Age of COVID-19," *Family Process* 59, no. 2 (June 2020): 1.
5. See David C. Dollahite et al., "Changes in Home-Centered Religious Practices and Relational Well-Being during the COVID-19 Pandemic," *Marriage & Family Review* (forthcoming); Heather H. Kelley et al., "Change in Financial Stress and Relational Wellbeing during COVID-19: Exacerbating and Alleviating Influences," *Journal of Family and Economic Issues*, published ahead of print, February 9, 2022, https://doi.org/10.1007/s10834-022-09822-7; Heather H. Kelley et al., "Changes in Spiritual Practices and Relational Well-Being during the COVID-19 Pandemic," *Marriage & Family Review*, published ahead of print, February 27, 2022, https://doi.org/10.1080/01494929.2021.2022563; Loren D. Marks et al., "Exploring COVID-19's Influence on Family Communication: Negative, Positive, or Both?," *Marriage & Family Review* (forthcoming); and Loren D. Marks et al., "Family Dinners and Family Relationships following the Initial Onset of the COVID-19 Pandemic," *Marriage & Family Review* (forthcoming).
6. See Pauline Boss, *Family Stress Management: A Contextual Approach* (Thousand Oaks, CA: SAGE, 2002).
7. See Amber J. Hammons and Barbara H. Fiese, "Is Frequency of Shared Family Meals Related to the Nutritional Health of Children and Adolescents?," *Pediatrics* 127, no. 6 (2011): 1565–74.
8. See Emma Armstrong-Carter and Eva H. Telzer, "Family Meals Buffer the Daily Emotional Risk Associated with Family Conflict," *Developmental Psychology* 56, no. 11 (2020): 2110–20.
9. See Ellie Lee et al., *Parenting Culture Studies* (London: Palgrave Macmillan, 2014).
10. See Nancy Eisenberg et al., "The Relations of Effortful Control and Impulsivity to Children's Resiliency and Adjustment," *Child Development* 75, no. 1 (2004): 25–46.
11. See Barbara H. Fiese et al., "A Review of 50 Years of Research on Naturally Occurring Family Routines and Rituals: Cause for Celebration?," *Journal of Family Psychology* 16, no. 4 (2002): 381–90; Barbara H. Fiese, Kimberly P. Foley, and Mary Spagnola, "Routine and Ritual Elements in Family Mealtimes: Contexts for Child Well-Being and Family Identity," *New Directions for Child and Adolescent Development*, no. 111 (Spring 2006): 67–89; and Barbara H. Fiese, Blake L. Jones, and Jaclyn A. Saltzman, "Systems Unify Family Psychology," in *APA Handbook of Contemporary Family Psychology*, ed. Barbara H. Fiese, vol. 1, *Foundations, Methods, and Contemporary Issues across the Lifespan* (Washington, DC: American Psychological Association, 2019).
12. See Marks et al., "Family Dinners."
13. For global COVID-19 rates of infections and deaths, see "Template:COVID-19 Pandemic Data," Wikipedia, updated May 2, 2022, https://en.wikipedia.org/wiki/Template:COVID-19_pandemic_data.
14. Quoted in Sarah Jane Weaver, "Revelation Guided 'an Interlocking Pattern of Strength' That Now Sustains the Church during COVID-19, Elder Cook Says," *Church News*, updated April 29, 2020, https://www.thechurchnews.com/leaders

-and-ministry/2020-04-29/coronavirus-elder-cook-revelation-home-centered-church-ministering-182549.
15. "Facts and Statistics," accessed May 2, 2022, newsroom.ChurchofJesusChrist.org.

CHAPTER TEN

Enjoying Revelatory Experiences in Family Relationships

In this chapter we offer some thoughts regarding enjoying revelatory experiences in marriage and family relationships, including across multiple generations (for example, between grandparents and grandchildren).

SEEKING AND RECEIVING ALL THE BEST SPIRITUAL GIFTS

Revelatory experiences involve communing with the Father, in the name of the Son, by the power of the Holy Spirit. Each of us has spiritual gifts that can help facilitate this communion (see Doctrine and Covenants 46:9–12). Further, our spiritual gifts can assist us in fulfilling whatever the Lord might call us to do based on our revelatory experiences.

The Lord revealed important principles on spiritual gifts to the Prophet Joseph Smith, which are recorded in Doctrine and Covenants section 46. These principles can help us as we seek to enjoy personal and interpersonal revelatory experiences in a home and family setting. On seeking spiritual gifts the Lord taught, "Wherefore, beware lest ye are deceived; and that you may not be deceived seek ye earnestly the *best gifts*, always remembering for what they are given" (Doctrine and Covenants 46:8; emphasis added). The fact that spiritual gifts from the Lord can help us avoid deception is comforting. Today inaccurate information prevails in our information-overloaded world, where false and inadequately contextualized information abounds about every subject imaginable, including the restored gospel and the Church. That the Lord uses the phrase "best gifts" in referring to spiritual gifts and commands us not just to seek them but to seek them earnestly suggests that we should devote great attention to seeking spiritual gifts such as faith, knowledge, wisdom, and healing (of body, spirit, mind, heart, and relationships).

About these "best gifts" the Lord then says, "For verily I say unto you, they are given for the benefit of those who love me and keep all my commandments, and him that seeketh so to do; that all may be benefited that seek or that ask of me" (Doctrine and Covenants 46:9). Note that it does not say that these best gifts are available only to those who keep all the commandments; rather, they are also for the benefit of those who seek to keep them. That the Lord states that all who seek and ask for these gifts "may be benefited" is a clear sign of God's abundant love, overflowing kindness, and abiding mercy for all His children. Perfection is not required to obtain these spiritual gifts nor to benefit from them—but effort and intent are.

The divine pattern of teaching by repeating important ideas is manifest in the next three verses:

> And again, verily I say unto you, I would that ye should *always remember*, and *always retain* in your minds what those gifts are, that are given unto the church.
>
> For all have not every gift given unto them; for there are *many gifts*, and to every man is given a gift by the Spirit of God.
>
> To some is given one, and to some is given another, *that all may be profited* thereby. (Doctrine and Covenants 46:10–12; emphasis added)

When the Lord desires that we "always remember" and "always retain" something in our minds, it likely is something of great importance. He desires that we always remember what those best gifts are, that there are many gifts, and that the gifts are given "that all may be profited." In a relational context, family members can help each other identify, appreciate, and nurture the spiritual gifts that the Lord has given to each family member. It is common for people not to be aware of their own spiritual gifts. Family members can be a great aid in helping each other recognize and develop spiritual gifts and share those with each other. In the next several verses (verses 13–29), the Lord lists many spiritual gifts, including knowledge, faith, wisdom, healing and being healed, miracles, prophecy, discerning of spirits, speaking with tongues, interpretation of tongues, and discerning all gifts.

Elder Bednar's teaching that revelation is "scattered among us"[1] is consistent with the Lord's teaching in section 46 that all have gifts but "to some is given one, and to some is given another" (verse 12). This suggests that each family who wants to enjoy more spiritual gifts should recognize, cultivate, and honor those diverse gifts that are "scattered among" or "given unto" different family members. It is important that parents don't seek to direct their children in all things but rather seek to help them cultivate their spiritual gifts, encourage them to seek inspiration from the Lord, and honor their moral agency as they exercise their spiritual gifts.

GRANDPARENTS AND REVELATORY EXPERIENCES

Grandparents have a unique opportunity to help turn the hearts of their grandchildren to the Lord and to encourage and facilitate their grandchildren's revelatory experiences. Most grandparents profoundly love and cherish their grandchildren. In turn, partly because most grandparents are not involved in the day-to-day monitoring and disciplining of their grandchildren, there often exists an especially close relational bond wherein grandchildren love, trust, and cherish their grandparents.

This bond allows grandparents to connect with their grandchildren on a deep level. Grandchildren love to hear their grandparents share stories from "the old days" and from their lives and adventures. This love opens doors for grandparents, as so inspired, to relate their sacred revelatory experiences with their grandchildren in ways that can profoundly influence them. Grandparents can share their stories of conversion, mission experiences, miracles in their lives (small and great ones), answered prayers, and the many ways the Lord has blessed them.

Grandparents who engage with their grandchildren about their spiritual and religious lives may be able to nurture their spiritual growth, answer (or encourage patience with) hard questions, provide the perspective of many decades of life, and provide a unique spiritual and religious resource that even the most devoted and loving parents might not be able to provide.

Grandparents often have more resources and more time (if not more energy) than parents and can make time to take grandchildren on religious "pilgrimages" to sacred religious places (such as temples or historical sites) and events (such as general conference). Grandchildren are likely to cherish and long remember such trips and events with their grandparents.

Grandparents can also take advantage of having more time and perspective to record their sacred revelatory experiences in writing, on audio or videotape, or in other creative ways. Until grandchildren are older, they may not be as interested in what their parents have to say or write but likely will be interested in records created by their beloved grandparents.

In addition, grandchildren can assist their grandparents in recording their sacred experiences by interviewing them about their lives—including their religious lives—and by helping them upload these interviews to FamilySearch or other online resources.

In sum, grandparents have an important and influential role in sharing and promoting revelatory experiences with the rising generation.

BUILDING ZION AND REVELATORY EXPERIENCES

We can think of our families as core building blocks of a Zion society. Because the Lord strongly desires that we build up Zion,[2] it is likely that being engaged as families in the building of Zion will result in profound revelatory experiences. Elder D. Todd Christofferson taught:

> Zion is Zion because of the character, attributes, and faithfulness of her citizens. Remember, "the Lord called his people Zion, because they were of one heart and one mind, and dwelt in righteousness; and there was no poor among them" (Moses 7:18). *If we would establish Zion in our homes*, branches, wards, and stakes, we must rise to this standard.

It will be necessary (1) to become unified in one heart and one mind; (2) to become, individually and collectively, a holy people; and (3) to care for the poor and needy with such effectiveness that we eliminate poverty among us. We cannot wait until Zion comes for these things to happen—Zion will come only as they happen.[3]

When we seek to faithfully facilitate revelatory experiences in our homes and families, we are more likely to grow in unity, holiness, and charity and thus are more likely to build Zion in our homes and broader communities. Similarly, if we strive to build Zion in our homes and families, we are more likely to be blessed with revelatory experiences that can assist us in our Zion-building efforts.

We are *Latter-day* Saints who are engaged in preparing ourselves, our children, and other loved ones for the Second Coming of the Lord Jesus Christ. The scriptures teach that the Second Coming will involve "the saints that are upon the earth" (Doctrine and Covenants 88:96) and "they who have slept in their graves" (Doctrine and Covenants 88:97) uniting with the Savior. Thus we can assume that family members from various generations will be with Christ as He begins His millennial reign on earth.

REVELATORY EXPERIENCES IN FAMILY HISTORY AND TEMPLE WORK

Families are close communities in which a relatively small number of people maintain close relationships, typically over the lifetime of the members. In the case of Latter-day Saint families, these communities also include ancestors now on the other side of the veil. That we do family history and work in sacred temples to bind family members together is clear evidence that our family communities transcend earthly and mortal boundaries. Many family members enjoy sacred revelatory experiences while doing family history and temple work, so families who do this work together will likely be able to enjoy sharing more profound revelatory experiences. Families are also sacred communities in which sacred meanings, sacred activities, sacred work, sacred sacrifices, and sacred relationships are part and parcel of family life.

Of the two authors of this book, Dave is an adult convert to The Church of Jesus Christ of Latter-day Saints and has had the marvelous blessing of being involved in family history and temple work for several members of his family that he personally knew and loved. Dave and his wife, Mary, served as proxies for Dave's grandparents and parents in the temple. About a year after Dave's sister Lana passed away, Dave and Mary went to the temple with two of their children, Camilla and Jonathan, to do the work for Lana. Lana was nine years older than Dave, and Camilla is about nine years older than Jonathan. Jonathan baptized and confirmed Camilla, who was acting on behalf of Lana, and Dave felt a strong sense that Lana was present and appreciative during the confirmation. Shared sacred experiences such as these might well be called shared revelatory experiences.

COUNCILS AND RELATIONAL REVELATORY EXPERIENCES

For decades, Elder M. Russell Ballard, among other leaders, has emphasized the importance of stake, ward, and family councils and has striven to elevate how the Saints meet and work together. Councils are used in communities of various sizes and purposes (for example, town councils, city councils, and ward councils). Any well-functioning community will have ways to share information and make important decisions, and councils facilitate this. But communities need more than decision-making bodies. They need ways to communicate and reinforce shared values and purposes, honor the past, honor achievement, celebrate meaningful events, work together, provide service to those in need, and have fun together.

People often think of decision-making when they think of councils, but a well-functioning council is about far more than decisions. Similarly, though it is wise to seek revelation during decision-making processes, revelation is about far more than decision-making. Many revelations and revelatory experiences (perhaps even most) shed light on identity, truth, vision, purpose, and relationships. A prime example of this is captured in the composition of the Doctrine and Covenants. In that book of revelations from the beginning of the Restoration, while some of the sections deal largely with decision-making (for example, sections 20, 84, and 107), many of the revelations are about giving Joseph and the early Saints additional light, truth, and knowledge about eternal things (for example, sections 45, 76, 88, 93, and 133).

If, as a part of regular couple and family councils or in home evenings, couples and families take time to discuss the importance of revelatory experiences and encourage each other in seeking, receiving, sharing, and recording personal, interpersonal, and shared revelatory experiences, these discussions likely will help encourage additional experiences in the future.

SACRED MATTERS: WHO, WHAT, WHY, WHERE, AND HOW

Just as there are many spiritual gifts, there are many kinds of revelatory experiences. The scriptural examples of people such as Adam and Eve, Enoch, Abraham, Moses, Lehi, Nephi, Alma, Enos, and Mary, the mother of Jesus, indicate that during revelatory experiences the Lord often opens new vistas, reveals eternal truths (particularly about the divine nature and destiny of the person receiving the revelatory experience), provides purpose and direction, pours out divine grace and mercy, and reveals the profound love that God has for that person and for all people.

Most of what the Lord desires to communicate to us in revelatory experiences can include matters around who, what, why, where, when, and how:

- "Who" matters might include who matters most (that is, God and Jesus), who God really is, who we really are, who our loved ones really are, and whom we might try to bless.
- "What" matters might include what matters most in this life; what we might do with our time, treasure, and talents; what we can do to commune with God; and what God would have us learn.
- "Why" matters might include why we are here, why God loves all His children, why we should seek to know the will of God, and why our marriage and family relationships matter so deeply.
- "Where" matters might include where we are going in this life, where we might find the truth and comfort we seek, where we might find the answers to our deepest and most troubling questions, and where we can turn for peace.
- "When" matters might include when to seek guidance, when to do various activities, when to best gather with loved ones, and when to express love and appreciation for others.
- "How" matters might include how we can relate to God, how we can relate to others, how we can be forgiven, how we can obtain comfort, how we can build strong relationships with others, how we might reconcile with others, how we can come to know God better, how we can live authentically in

relation to others, how we can express love and appreciation for others, how we can lift the hands and strengthen the feeble knees of others (see Doctrine and Covenants 81:5), and how we can best serve the Lord and others.

When we approach God about a decision, we often want to know what He wants us to do. However, God has made it clear that He wants to honor our agency, to help us make decisions, and to encourage us to be anxiously engaged in good causes of our "own free will" (Doctrine and Covenants 58:28; see verses 27, 29). While He will frequently confirm our decisions or caution us, He does not want to make decisions for us. He does not want us to be puppets, trained animals, automatons, or slaves. We begin our spiritual journeys as His children and are His disciples and servants. However, based on the scriptures, it is clear that He desires to consider and call us His friends (see John 15:15; Doctrine and Covenants 84:77).

FAITH, HOPE, AND CHARITY IN ENJOYING REVELATORY EXPERIENCES

In Latter-day Saint Sunday meetings, when we speak about revelation, we understandably focus on the important role of faith. Faith in the Lord Jesus Christ is the first principle of the gospel and is a primary principle of receiving revelation. Faith is also important in a home-centered approach to enjoying personal and interpersonal revelatory experiences. In addition, we suggest that when we are thinking, writing, and speaking with one another about how to enjoy personal and interpersonal revelatory experiences more often—especially about sharing revelatory experiences in our homes and families—it may be just as important to focus on the other two virtues that Paul discusses in 1 Corinthians 13: hope and charity.

HOPE AND ENJOYING REVELATORY EXPERIENCES

The Church's online resource Gospel Topics has some wonderful and applicable ideas on the power of hope:

> As we strive to live the gospel, we grow in our ability to "abound in hope, through the power of the Holy Ghost" (Romans 15:13). We increase in hope as we pray and seek God's forgiveness. . . .

The principle of hope extends into the eternities, but it also can sustain us through the everyday challenges of life. "Happy is he," said the Psalmist, "that hath the God of Jacob for his help, whose hope is in the Lord his God" (Psalm 146:5). With hope, we can find joy in life. We can "have patience, and bear with . . . afflictions, with a firm hope that ye shall one day rest from all your afflictions" (Alma 34:41). We can "press forward with a steadfastness in Christ, having a perfect brightness of hope, and a love of God and of all men. Wherefore, if ye shall press forward, feasting upon the word of Christ, and endure to the end, behold, thus saith the Father: Ye shall have eternal life" (2 Nephi 31:20).[4]

When "through the power of the Holy Ghost" we enjoy revelatory experiences, our hope increases until we "abound in hope," which allows us to better "press forward with a steadfastness in Christ" in all we do. In the processes of sharing personal and interpersonal revelatory experiences in a family context, the importance of hope is magnified.

CHARITY AND ENJOYING REVELATORY EXPERIENCES

Charity is an essential element in enjoying revelatory experiences in the home and family context. Paul stated that faith, hope, and charity all abound but that charity is the greatest of these three virtues (see 1 Corinthians 13:13). Charity, or "the pure love of Christ" (Moroni 7:47), is also the greatest virtue when we enjoy, experience, and share sacred and personal things with others. When love abounds during sacred family gatherings (for example, family prayer, family scripture study, and home evening), it is more likely that family members will feel the Holy Spirit and thus be more likely to enjoy personal and family revelatory experiences. When love abounds in marital and family relationships, then during marital and family conversations, it is more likely that spouses or family members will be willing to convey deeply personal thoughts, feelings, and experiences. When love abounds during family activities (for example, family chores, vacations, recreational activities, or board games), it is more likely that family members will feel the unity, joy, and safety that often are a prerequisite for relating deeply personal or sacred things with others.

When someone lets us onto their sacred ground by sharing something sacred or deeply personal, they are giving us a treasured gift. It is an act of love. Thus a person who is on the receiving end of a family member sharing something sacred or personal likely hopes to know how to best understand and how to best respond with love and kindness. Hope and love thus join with faith in encouraging sharing sacred revelatory experiences in homes and families.

REVELATION IN FAMILY RELATIONSHIPS

One important consideration of revelatory experiences in marriages and families concerns timing and sharing. To what extent do people in couples or families receive the same message from the Lord at the same time? We are not aware of any research on this question, and we have not had extensive discussions about this question with many married Latter-day Saint couples. However, we both discussed this issue with our wives, Sandra and Mary. Our marriages may be different from others, but in about sixty-six years of combined marriage (more than twenty-six for Loren and Sandra; nearly forty for Dave and Mary), our experience is that it is exceedingly rare to obtain what might be called "synchronous revelation," when both the wife and the husband receive the same clear revelation at the same time and in the same way. It has been far more frequent for one spouse to receive inspiration and then share it with the other spouse, who later receives confirmation (in his or her own time and own way), as illustrated in the following examples that our wives have approved for sharing.

SANDRA AND LOREN'S EXPERIENCE

In the summer of 2007, Sandra called me from several states away and said, "Are you sitting down? If not, you probably need to."

"OK, I'm now planted on the couch," I responded.

"Loren, I thought we were done having children, but I keep getting the overwhelming prompting that there is a little girl up there for us and that she will be named after her two great-grandmothers," Sandra said.

After a period of mild shock that lasted somewhere between days and weeks, I felt a clear confirmation. Such experiences might be called "asynchronous revelation," or the same directions but with different timing.

Our daughter Aliyah JodyMarie was born on June 10, 2008. Aliyah means "blessing," while Jody and Marie are names borrowed from one maternal great-grandmother and one paternal great-grandmother. Over the years, we have been struck by how many of our dear friends and family members have had revelatory experiences (whether synchronous or asynchronous) regarding bringing children into the world, including Mary and Dave Dollahite.

MARY AND DAVE'S EXPERIENCE

Mary and I also have had very few experiences with synchronous revelation in our married life. One of the few was about the birth of our seventh child. When we were first married, I asked Mary how many children she wanted to have. She said she did not have some number of children decided on ahead of time, and she expected they would come "one child at a time." That is what our children did. When we had six children, we thought our family might be complete. Mary was forty years old and nursing child number six on demand. We were open to more children but not necessarily expecting to add another member to our family.

Then, several times, when we called the family together for prayer, the feeling that someone was missing was experienced simultaneously. At least two times this occurred when people other than immediate family were present. Those others voiced the feeling. Once when some dear family friends were visiting, we had all gathered in a circle for family prayer, and our friend Peg Lewis said it felt like someone was missing. Another time, not long after, it happened again when Mary's sister Sarah was visiting. When all had gathered in a circle for family prayer, Sarah said it seemed like someone was missing. Both times we counted the children and found all accounted for. Both Mary and I felt like God was sending a strong message. Mary was almost forty-two when our last child was born.

REVELATION YIELDS LIFE

As marvelous as revelation can be, it is not an "end"—it is a means. It is an essential part of the covenant path. In the two personal and familial stories we shared, revelatory experiences literally yielded life. Similarly, the ultimate purpose of revelatory experiences is to yield eternal life, or, phrased differently, to help us build eternal families through Christ.

As we discuss at the outset of the book and throughout it, faithfully studying the scriptures (for example, through the *Come, Follow Me* invitation) is vital not so that we can check the "been there, read that" box but because, as President Nelson has taught, faithful study is an ideal way to accentuate our ability to hear Jesus Christ.[5] In direct terms, faithful study of the words of both ancient and modern prophets promotes revelatory experiences, and revelatory experiences can help our families make it back to our eternal home.

In charting our course home, we must hold to the rod—including God's commandments and our covenants. David A. Bednar raised two essential issues about receiving personal revelation:

> *It is vitally important to always remember that the Holy Ghost will NOT prompt an individual to violate sacred covenants and disobey God's commandments.*
>
> *The Spirit of the Lord will NOT prompt any person to think or act in a manner that is contrary to the doctrine and the authorized practices of the Savior's restored Church* as contained in the holy scriptures.[6]

PRODIGAL CHILDREN AND RELATIONAL RECONCILIATION

In an online gospel study group that one of us participated in, many parents discussed an increasing sense of anxiety about their ability to teach their children the gospel in a way that would inoculate them against the many dangerous spiritual and philosophical viruses populating dominant culture and the internet. The internet has so many ideas, images, programs, and philosophies that are spiritually, psychologically, and relationally harmful that many parents feel as if they can be as diligent as possible in their parenting and still "lose their children to the world." We both sympathize and empathize.

One mother and therapist has mentioned that based on her experience, she has come to believe that one vitally important skill for parents to develop is the willingness and ability to reconcile with and forgive their children. Nearly all Latter-day Saint parents will find that at least one of their children will at some point make choices that distance the child from God, the gospel, and the family. Like the forgiving father in the parable of the prodigal son (see Luke 15:11–32), such parents actively and patiently wait for their children to make any movement back home to God and family, then quickly forgive them and enthusiastically welcome them home.[7] Indeed, we believe that knowing how to best go about reconciling with children who have, in one way or another, turned away from their parents or their parents' faith is among the most important of all parenting skills. It is also among perhaps the most complex and challenging skills—perhaps so challenging that it cannot be done well without hearing Him who would be the mender of all breaches through His "At-one-ment."

We do not have simple, formulaic, or guaranteed advice except to strive to live basic gospel principles such as seeking and following the Spirit, being humble and kind, being patient and long-suffering, and following Moroni's counsel about charity to "pray unto the Father with all the energy of heart, that ye may be filled with this love" (Moroni 7:48).

In other words, as we love and labor with our children who have distanced themselves from us and our beliefs and values, we should strive to be as our Heavenly Father and our Savior are with us. The essence of Their eternal work is to bear with us in our sins and help us reconcile ourselves to Them. In doing this, They have suffered for and with us, have sacrificed for us, and always stand with open arms and hearts to receive us when we move back to Them.

QUESTIONS TO ENCOURAGE CONTEMPLATION AND CONVERSATION

1. What spiritual gifts have you and your family members received from the Lord, and how are you using those spiritual gifts?
2. Did your own grandparents share revelatory experiences with you? If you are a grandparent, how can you share revelatory experiences with your grandchildren?
3. How have your own revelatory experiences encouraged you to build Zion?
4. What revelatory experiences have you and your loved ones enjoyed from participating in family history and temple work?
5. How have you seen stake, ward, or family councils facilitate revelatory experiences?

6. What has been your experience with loved ones in terms of the timing of revelatory experiences? Have you and your loved ones enjoyed any synchronous revelations?

7. What are the main takeaway messages you have received from the Spirit as you have read this book?

CREATING OPPORTUNITIES FOR REVELATORY EXPERIENCES (CORE)

1. What intentions do you have to enjoy personal revelatory experiences?
2. How can you and your loved ones encourage each other's revelatory experiences?
3. What personal and relational activities might encourage your own revelatory experiences?

NOTES

1. David A. Bednar, *The Spirit of Revelation* (Salt Lake City: Deseret Book, 2021), 57–60.
2. See "Enrichment B: Establishing Zion," in *Doctrine and Covenants Student Manual* (Salt Lake City: The Church of Jesus Christ of Latter-day Saints, 2002), 369–74.
3. D. Todd Christofferson, "Come to Zion," *Ensign*, November 2008, 38; emphasis added.
4. Gospel Topics, "Hope," topics.ChurchofJesusChrist.org.
5. See Russell M. Nelson, "Hear Him," *Ensign*, May 2020, 89–92.
6. Bednar, *Spirit of Revelation*, 37; emphasis in original.
7. See Desmond Tutu and Mpho Tutu, *The Book of Forgiving: The Fourfold Path for Healing Ourselves and Our World* (New York: HarperOne, 2014).

CHAPTER ELEVEN

Revelation and Home-Centered Ways of Gathering Covenant Israel

This book has focused on two of the major themes of President Russell M. Nelson's prophetic ministry—personal revelation and home-centered religious life. In this concluding chapter, we will briefly discuss two other central themes that the living prophet has emphasized: (a) the gathering of Israel and (b) the central importance of covenants and "the covenant path." We will first share prophetic teachings and scriptural verses pertaining to the gathering of Israel and then will suggest ways that Latter-day Saints can seek and share revelatory experiences as they fulfill these prophetic calls in their homes and families.

THE GATHERING OF ISRAEL

In a 2006 general conference talk, while serving as an Apostle, President Russell M. Nelson said, "We are part of a great movement—the gathering of scattered Israel. I speak of this doctrine today because of its unique importance in God's eternal plan." He then taught about the importance of the "doctrine of the gathering":

> This doctrine of the gathering is one of the important teachings of The Church of Jesus Christ of Latter-day Saints. The Lord has declared: "I give unto you a sign . . . that I shall gather in, from their long dispersion, my people, O house of Israel, and shall establish again among them my Zion" [3 Nephi 21:1]. . . . We not only teach this doctrine, but we participate in it. We do so as we help to gather the elect of the Lord on both sides of the veil.[1]

Since becoming the Lord's prophet, President Nelson has put even greater emphasis on the gathering of Israel. In a landmark talk to the youth of the worldwide Church, he taught about the importance of the gathering of Israel and referenced teachings about it in the Book of Mormon.[2] In the first book of the Book of Mormon, the prophet Nephi teaches about the gathering of Israel in the last days:

> And after the house of Israel should be scattered they should be gathered together again; or, in fine, after the Gentiles had received the fulness of the Gospel, the natural branches of the olive tree, or the remnants of the house of Israel, should be grafted in, or come to the knowledge of the true Messiah, their Lord and their Redeemer. (1 Nephi 10:14)

Nephi taught that the purpose of the gathering of Israel centers on people receiving a knowledge of the true Messiah, the Lord Jesus Christ. Then, in 3 Nephi, that true Messiah, the resurrected Savior, taught that the coming forth of the Book of Mormon would be "a sign" to those in the latter days "that ye may know the time when these things shall be about to take place—that I shall gather in, from their long dispersion, my people, O house of Israel, and shall establish again among them my Zion" (3 Nephi 21:1). The Savior taught that the gathering of Israel (or Jacob) involves the establishment of Zion.

In his talk to the youth of Zion, President Nelson emphasized the importance of the gathering of Israel in the lives of each young man and young woman:

> My dear young brothers and sisters, these surely *are* the latter days, and the Lord is hastening His work to gather Israel. That gathering is the most important thing taking place on earth today. Nothing else compares in magnitude, nothing else compares in importance, nothing else compares in majesty. . . .
>
> My dear extraordinary youth, you were sent to earth at this precise time, the most crucial time in the history of the world, to help gather Israel. There is *nothing* happening on this earth right now that is more important than that. There is *nothing* of greater consequence. Absolutely *nothing*.
>
> This gathering should mean *everything* to you. This is the mission for which you were sent to earth. . . .
>
> *Anytime* you do *anything* that helps *anyone*—on either side of the veil—take a step toward making covenants with God and receiving their essential baptismal and temple ordinances, you are helping to gather Israel.[3]

In a 2018 general conference talk to the women of the Church, President Nelson taught about the ways that women can help gather Israel:

> It is a cause that desperately needs women, because women shape the future. So tonight I'm extending a prophetic plea to you, the women of the Church, to shape the future by helping to gather scattered Israel. . . .
>
> My dear sisters, we need *you*! We "need *your* strength, *your* conversion, *your* conviction, *your* ability to lead, *your* wisdom, and *your* voices."[4] We simply cannot gather Israel without you.[5]

Turning from the words of our modern prophet, President Nelson, to an ancient one, we read the following words of Mormon in 3 Nephi 5 as he prophesied of the last days and the gathering of Israel (whose birth name was Jacob):

> And as surely as the Lord liveth, will he gather in from the four quarters of the earth all the remnant of the seed of Jacob, who are scattered abroad upon all the face of the earth.
>
> And as he hath *covenanted* with all the house of Jacob, even so shall the *covenant* wherewith he hath *covenanted* with the house of Jacob be fulfilled in his own due time, unto the restoring all the house of Jacob unto *the knowledge of the covenant that he hath covenanted with them.*
>
> And then shall *they know their Redeemer, who is Jesus Christ, the Son of God*; and then shall they be gathered in from the four quarters of the earth unto their own lands, from whence they have been dispersed; yea, as the Lord liveth so shall it be. Amen. (Verses 24–26; emphasis added)

In this passage, Mormon references "covenant" or "covenanted" five times to help us understand the centrality of covenants. Also note that Mormon uses the word "all" repeatedly in these verses (he uses "all the remnant" and "all the face of the earth" once and "all the house of Jacob" twice).

THE CENTRAL IMPORTANCE OF COVENANTS AND "THE COVENANT PATH"

Few phrases are more closely tied to President Nelson than his loving counsel to "keep on the covenant path."[6] Elder D. Todd Christofferson summarized, "Throughout his ministry, President Russell M. Nelson has studied and taught of God's covenants with His children. He is himself a shining example of one who walks the covenant path."[7]

In fact, in his first message as President of the Church, President Nelson stated:

> Your commitment to follow the Savior by making covenants with Him and then keeping those covenants will open the door to every spiritual blessing and privilege available to men, women, and children everywhere.
> . . . The ordinances of the temple and the covenants you make there are key to strengthening your life, your marriage and family, and your ability to resist the attacks of the adversary. Your worship in the

temple and your service there for your ancestors will bless you with increased personal revelation and peace and will fortify your commitment to stay on the covenant path.[8]

Covenants are sometimes thought of as being profoundly personal and individual—and in some senses they are. However, the impact of making and keeping covenants is expansive and eternal. The power of covenants, when honored, can shake and shape both time and eternity. The late Apostle Elder John A. Widtsoe referred to covenants as world changing: "The world moves forward by the efforts of covenanted people—*who keep their covenants.*"[9] Indeed, the solemn power of honored covenants extends forward and backward in time, across generations, and on both sides of the veil. It is to these realities that we now turn. And yet these monumental possibilities begin in the humble setting of home and family. That is, while the gathering of Israel has global reach and while the covenant path extends through eternity, small and simple actions in our personal and relational lives allow us to contribute to these grand endeavors (see Alma 37:6).

BLESSING FAMILIES BY TURNING HEARTS

Two powerful divine promises found in the first and the last books of the Old Testament have great relevance to covenant making, to covenant keeping, and to the gathering of Israel on both sides of the veil. In Genesis 12:3 the Lord promises Abraham, "And I will bless them that bless thee, and curse him that curseth thee: and in thee shall all families of the earth be blessed." Again, note the use of the word "all" in this promise. The scope of this divine promise includes all the history of the earth as well as eternity. The Book of Abraham provides clarification to this promise that the seed of Abraham includes his actual descendants, his "literal seed," as well as those who receive the gospel covenant and are "called after [his] name" (Abraham 2:10). So all the seed of Abraham will be a blessing to all families of the earth.

In the last book of the Old Testament, the Lord makes another promise:

> Behold, I will send you Elijah the prophet before the coming of the great and dreadful day of the Lord:

And he shall turn the heart of the fathers to the children, and the heart of the children to their fathers, lest I come and smite the earth with a curse. (Malachi 4:5–6)

This promise is of such profound importance that it is repeated nearly verbatim in the Doctrine and Covenants at least half a dozen times (see sections 2, 27, 98, 110, 128, and 138), in the Pearl of Great Price (see Joseph Smith—History 1:39), and in the Book of Mormon by the Savior Himself (see 3 Nephi 25:5–6). The fulfillment of the great promises involving keys, covenants, gathering, and turning hearts has commenced.

Along with the "dispensation of the gospel of Abraham," the keys to the gathering of Israel on earth and in eternity were revealed when the Kirtland Temple was dedicated and Moses, Elias, and Elijah appeared to the Prophet Joseph Smith:

After this vision closed, the heavens were again opened unto us; and Moses appeared before us, and committed unto us the keys of the gathering of Israel from the four parts of the earth, and the leading of the ten tribes from the land of the north.

After this, Elias appeared, and committed the dispensation of the gospel of Abraham, saying that in us and our seed all generations after us should be blessed.

After this vision had closed, another great and glorious vision burst upon us; for Elijah the prophet, who was taken to heaven without tasting death, stood before us, and said:

Behold the time has fully come, which was spoken of by the mouth of Malachi—testifying that he [Elijah] should be sent, before the great and dreadful day of the Lord come—

To turn the heart of the fathers to the children, and the children to the fathers, lest the whole earth be smitten with a curse—

Therefore, the keys of this dispensation are committed into your hands; and by this ye may know that the great and dreadful day of the Lord is near, even at the doors. (Doctrine and Covenants 110:11–16)

About this, President Nelson taught:

> The Lord reaffirmed the Abrahamic covenant in our day through the Prophet Joseph Smith. In the temple we receive our ultimate blessings, as the seed of Abraham, Isaac, and Jacob. . . .
>
> . . . We gather pedigree charts, create family group sheets, and do temple work vicariously to gather individuals unto the Lord and into their families. . . .
>
> This work of Almighty God is true. He lives. Jesus is the Christ. This is His Church, restored to accomplish its divine destiny, including the promised gathering of Israel.[10]

IMPLICATIONS OF THE PROPHET'S TEACHINGS

We find it meaningful that, in teaching about the gathering of Israel, both the Lord Jesus Christ and His prophets, ancient and modern, have used decisive terms (such as *all*, *nothing*, *everything*, *anytime*, *anything*, and *anyone*). This gives us some sense of the deep importance, meaning, and purpose of the gathering. This strength and urgency of language is appropriate because the gathering of Israel is about inviting *every* person to receive the knowledge of his or her Savior and Redeemer and to make saving and exalting covenants with Him. Latter-day Saints can enjoy these ultimate blessings during their life on earth and are able to help extend these blessings to those on the other side of the veil. Because God blesses those who seek to bless others in His family in this way, this work is indeed among the most satisfying and consequential work on earth.

President Nelson urged the youth in the Church to deeply ponder, pray, and counsel together about how they might gather covenant Israel.[11] Likewise, Latter-day Saint parents and grandparents—and future grandparents—would do well to think about how they might assist and encourage their children and grandchildren in this shared sacred mission. Stake and ward leaders might also consider how they can support the parents and grandparents in their stakes and wards in this mighty work.

A question from *Come, Follow Me* asks, "What do I feel inspired to do to help fulfill the promise that 'all the families of the earth shall be blessed'? (Abraham 2:11)."[12] We think this is a good question to ask ourselves. As an individual, none of us can bless *all* the families of earth. But as individuals, as couples, and as families, we can try to be a blessing to some families, beginning with our own and then branching out to help others. The Prophet Joseph Smith said:

> Love is one of the leading characteristics of Deity, and ou[gh]t to be manifested by those who aspire to be the Sons of God. A man filled with the love of God, is not content with blessing his family alone, but ranges through the world, anxious to bless the whole of the human family.[13]

We are greatly blessed in the latter days because we can use various technologies that virtually range through the world—from the comfort of our homes—to share the glorious truths of the restored gospel, do family history work, and provide humanitarian assistance to those in need.

GATHERING ENCOURAGES REVELATORY EXPERIENCES

Throughout history, the Lord has called His people to gather in various ways: in temples, in sacred gatherings, and in quorums and councils. Perhaps one of the most important purposes of gathering as covenant people is to receive revelatory experiences.

TEMPLES

The Prophet Joseph Smith taught that in every dispensation the Lord has gathered His people to build temples. Among other things, temples are places of revelation. In an informative essay on the Nephites gathering to the temple in Bountiful to hear the Savior, Gerald Hansen Jr. discussed the principle of gathering and revelation at the temple:

> "Gathering," in the highest sense of the word, means to receive the same temple blessings that Abraham received. Gathering to "lands" is primarily for the purpose of gathering to locations where we have or will build temples. As Joseph Smith said, the main object of gathering the people of God in any age to certain places is "to build unto the Lord a house whereby He could reveal unto His people the ordinances of His

house and the glories of His kingdom, and teach the people the way of salvation" (*Teachings of the Prophet Joseph Smith* 307–308).[14]

God gathers us to reveal to us divine ordinances, glories, and teachings. In this dispensation, from the outpouring of divine and angelic appearances in the Kirtland Temple in 1836 (see Doctrine and Covenants 110) to the outpouring of revelation regarding the priesthood received by the First Presidency and Quorum of the Twelve Apostles in 1978 (see Official Declaration 2), the Saints have received, as individuals and in groups, profound revelatory experiences when gathered in temples.

MEETINGS AND COUNCILS

Many Saints receive revelatory experiences when gathered with other Saints in sacrament meetings, Sunday School classes, Relief Society meetings, and priesthood meetings. Earlier in the book we noted Elder Bednar's teaching that a key purpose of our meetings and councils (at home and at church buildings) is to enjoy revelatory experiences together.[15] The Lord is always pouring out His Spirit on His Saints. Wherever we are, whatever we are doing, and whenever we are open to receive them, personal and interpersonal revelatory experiences are available to us. This is especially true in our meetings and councils, including home and family-centered gatherings, in which the combined faith of those gathered results in the Spirit being manifest in the hearts, minds, and spirits of the Saints. A central purpose of Church councils is for leaders to gather to receive revelation about the needs of those they serve. Likewise, a central purpose of couple and family councils is for family members to gather to enjoy personal and interpersonal revelatory experiences for the edification of all in the family as well as for others whom family members can influence and serve.

THE BLESSINGS OF BELIEF IN GOD AND HIS PROPHETS

The fourth king of Judah, Jehoshaphat, spoke to his people during stressful, dangerous times and pleaded with them to "believe in the Lord your God, so shall ye be established; believe his prophets, so shall ye prosper" (2 Chronicles 20:20). We concur with King Jehoshaphat that in all times, but particularly during changing and difficult times, believing in God and

God's prophets allows us to be established and to prosper in our homes and families. We urge all Latter-day Saints and all families of the earth to turn their hearts and minds and ears to the living God and His living prophets. We are confident that doing so will allow Zion to be established in each heart, in each family, and throughout all the earth so that when the Lord Jesus Christ returns to earth in glory, there will be a worldwide community of covenant Saints prepared to welcome Him as their King.

CONCLUSION

Years ago, a friend who was wary of a long-winded and preachy answer said, "All right, tell me what your church is all about—but in ten words or less." The response, after some deep reflection and quick counting, was "building eternal families through Christ."

Our core intent in this book is not simply to promote home-centered worship or to reissue the invitation to "come, follow me." It is not simply to highlight President Nelson's exhortation to seek revelation and to "hear Him." Our core intent is to support and sustain our living prophet and the Savior's Church in the sacred effort to build eternal families through Christ.

We have spent over a quarter of a century of our professional lives together, earnestly seeking answers and insights regarding how to build eternal families. Despite countless mistakes that we have made in our personal, familial, and professional efforts to build exemplary (and hopefully eternal) families, we humbly offer you some of the best of what we have learned. We share our personal witness that there is a potential in imperfect but sincere and faithful home-centered worship of the Father—a potential that refines our ability to welcome, recognize, hear, and respond to the power of God that flows through revelation. This revelation guides, lifts, directs, and heals us as we progress along the covenant path. Graciously and mercifully, this covenant path of faith, revelation, action, and Christ-inspired concern for others will lead us forward so that our home-centered efforts here will culminate in a joyous and eternal return "home to that God who gave [us] life" (Alma 40:11; see Helaman 3:29–30).

QUESTIONS TO ENCOURAGE CONTEMPLATION AND CONVERSATION

1. What aspects of the gathering of Israel are most important to you and your family members?
2. What personal and relational activities would be most likely to help you and your family stay on the covenant path?
3. What meaningful revelatory experiences have you enjoyed while gathered in your family or with the Saints?
4. What are some practical ways you could help turn the hearts of parents and children and of grandparents and grandchildren to one another?

CREATING OPPORTUNITIES FOR REVELATORY EXPERIENCES (CORE)

1. What intentions do you have to enjoy personal revelatory experiences?
2. How can you and your loved ones encourage each other's revelatory experiences?
3. What personal and relational activities might encourage your own revelatory experiences?

NOTES

1. Russell M. Nelson, "The Gathering of Scattered Israel," *Ensign*, November 2006, 79, 80.
2. See Russell M. Nelson and Wendy W. Nelson, "Hope of Israel" (worldwide youth devotional, June 3, 2018), note 7, https://abn.ChurchofJesusChrist.org/study/broadcasts/worldwide-devotional-for-young-adults/2018/06/hope-of-israel.
3. Nelson and Nelson, "Hope of Israel."
4. Russell M. Nelson, "A Plea to My Sisters," *Ensign*, November 2015, 96; emphasis added.
5. Russell M. Nelson, "Sisters' Participation in the Gathering of Israel," *Ensign*, November 2018, 69, 70.
6. Russell M. Nelson, "As We Go Forward Together," *Ensign*, April 2018, 7.
7. D. Todd Christofferson, "Why the Covenant Path," *Ensign*, May 2021, 116.
8. Nelson, "As We Go Forward Together," 7.
9. John A. Widtsoe, *Evidences and Reconciliations*, comp. G. Homer Durham (Salt Lake City: Bookcraft, 1960), 196–97.
10. Nelson, "Gathering of Scattered Israel," 80–81.
11. See Nelson and Nelson, "Hope of Israel."
12. *Come, Follow Me—For Individuals and Families: Old Testament 2022* (Salt Lake City: The Church of Jesus Christ of Latter-day Saints, 2021), 30.
13. Joseph Smith, "Letter to Quorum of the Twelve, 15 December 1840," p. 2, The Joseph Smith Papers, https://www.josephsmithpapers.org/paper-summary/letter-to-quorum-of-the-twelve-15-december-1840/2.

14. Gerald Hansen Jr., "Gathering to the Temple: Teachings of the Second Day," in *The Book of Mormon: 3 Nephi 9–30; This Is My Gospel*, ed. Monte S. Nyman and Charles D. Tate Jr. (Provo, UT: Religious Studies Center, Brigham Young University, 1993), 214.
15. See David A. Bednar, *The Spirit of Revelation* (Salt Lake City: Deseret Book, 2021), 58; see also Bednar, in "Panel Discussion" (worldwide leadership training meeting, November 2010), broadcasts.ChurchofJesusChrist.org.

Index

A
Abrams, Diane, 100
Abrams, Robert, 100
Abrahamic covenant, 183–85
Adam and Eve, 9–10, 25–27
adaptability, 59–60
agency, 59, 95, 128, 172
Alma the Younger, 70, 128
Andersen, Neil L., 51
apostles. *See* prophets and apostles
asynchronous revelation, 174–75

B
Ballard, M. Russell, 170
baptisms, during COVID-19 pandemic, 150
Bednar, David A., xvii, 2, 31–32, 36, 78, 148, 167, 176
bedtime routine, 40–41
Benjamin, King, address of, 27–29
blessing children, 107–10
Boss, Pauline, 151
branch members, closer connection with, 142–45
burnout, 120
Burr, Wes, 74

C
Chadwick, Bruce, 14
charity, in enjoying revelatory experiences, 173–74
children
  blessing, 107–10
  enthusiasm of, 122–27
  of exemplary families, 94
  expressing pride in, 108–10
  and family teaching pattern, 8–12, 25–26, 70
  formative years of, 71

children *(continued)*
    ideas and encouragement for families with older, 90–92
    ideas and encouragement for families with small, 88–90
    responsibility to teach, 95
    revelatory experiences regarding, 39–41, 174–75
    Sabbath observance and parents' relationship with, 111–12
    spiritual experiences for, 42–43
    wayward, 176–77
Christofferson, D. Todd, 12, 16, 168–69, 182
Church meetings, 120, 187
Church of Jesus Christ of Latter-day Saints, The
    emphasis on family in, 33
    features of millennials in, 35–36
    as home-centered church, 11–12
    religious practices during COVID-19 pandemic, 157–58
Coles, Robert, 117
Come, Follow Me. See also home-centered gospel living and learning; prophetic promises, fulfillment of
    ideas and encouragement regarding, 89–90, 91–92
    ideas for individual study of, 56–59
    implementation of, 54–55, 60
    members' recent experiences with, 61–62
    purpose of, 53
commandments, 65, 136, 143–44
communication, during COVID-19 pandemic, 154–55
comparison, 60
consecration, 5, 18, 53, 162
conversion
    caused by King Benjamin's address, 28
    deepened, 53
    home-centered gospel learning and lasting, 15–16, 30
    individual study and worship and lasting, 13–15
    pattern of, 70
    personal revelatory experience and, 35–37
    spiritual fire and, 34
Cook, Quentin L.
    on COVID-19 pandemic, 157
    on deepened conversion and faith, 52, 53
    on flexibility in implementing *Come, Follow Me*, 60
    on home-centered gospel learning, 12–13, 15–16
    on Jewish Sabbath observance, 100
    on media, 104–5
    on Sabbath, 99, 112
councils, 170–71, 187
covenant path, 64–65, 144–45, 157, 182–88
covenants, 143–44, 182–88
COVID-19 pandemic, 147–48, 161–62
    authors' experiences with home-centered learning during, 159–61
    family communication during, 154–55
    family meals during, 151–54
    family responses to, 149
    as growth opportunity, 156–57
    and home-centered learning, 148, 157–59
    religious practices during, 149–51
    takeaways regarding, 155–56
Coyne, Sarah, 104
Craig, Michelle D., 55
Craven, Becky, 52
"Creating Opportunities for Revelatory Experiences" (CORE), xvii
creativity, 59–60
crises, as growth opportunities, 156–57, 158

D

dancing, and Sabbath observance, 106
deception, 166
decision-making, 170, 172
divine discontent, 55
Doherty, William J., 18, 71, 76, 141
Dollahite, Camilla, 170
Dollahite, Jonathan, 170
Dollahite, Lana, 170
Dollahite, Mary, 170

E

effort, to increase faith, 30
electronic devices, 60, 104–5
Elias, 184
Elijah, 183–84
Emerson, Ralph Waldo, 57–58, 86
eternal life, 3, 12, 50, 65, 175–76
exemplary families, 17–19, 38–39, 62–64, 70–71, 74, 93–95

F

faith
    effort to increase, 30
    in enjoying revelatory experiences, 172
    and navigating trials, 38–39, 44
    personal revelatory experience and deepened, 35–37
    strengthened, 52
families
    challenges facing, 95–96
    communication in, during COVID-19 pandemic, 154–55
    conclusions regarding COVID-19 pandemic and, 161–62
    exemplary, 17–19, 38–39, 62–64, 70–71, 74, 93–95
    home-centered learning's impact on, 139–42
    importance of, 33
    religious practices of, during COVID-19 pandemic, 149–51
    responses of, to COVID-19 pandemic, 149
    revelation in family relationships, 165–77
    and Sabbath observance, 105–11
    and shared revelatory experiences, 27, 33–34
    teaching pattern in, 8–12, 25–26, 70
    as universally imperfect, 19–20
family gospel study, 69–74. *See also* shared revelatory experiences
    challenges of, 79–82
    ideas and encouragement regarding, 85–97
    realities concerning, 74–79

family history work, 169–70
family home evening. *See* home evening
family meals, 110–11, 151–54, 156
family prayer, 72–74, 152–54, 156
Fiese, Barbara, 152
fire, spiritual, 34
First Vision, 29, 34, 69
Flake, Kathleen, 34
flexibility, 16, 18, 59–60
Frankl, Viktor, 81
future, optimism for, 51, 96

G

generational loss, 35
generativity, 5. *See also* consecration
gifts of the Spirit, 165–67
God
    blessings of belief in, 187–88
    communing with, 64
    drawing closer to, 144–45
    and family teaching pattern, 8–10
    love of, 186
    personal relationship with, 36–37, 62–64, 70–71
    reality of, 37
    seeing others through perspective of, 39
Goddard, Wally, 7
Gottman, John, 130, 141
grandparents, 160–61, 167–68
Grant, Heber J., 57, 67n23
Greenberg, Blu, 101–2, 112

H

habits, forming, 57–58
Hansen, Gerald, Jr., 186–87
Haws, J. B., 60
hearts, turning, 183–85
heaven, homesickness for, 42
Heschel, Abraham Joshua, 102
Hinckley, Gordon B., 100
Holland, Jeffrey R., 35
Holy Ghost, 16, 32, 137–39
home
    importance of gospel learning in, 79
    sacredness of, 33–34, 95
home-centered gospel living and learning. *See also Come, Follow Me*;

family gospel study; individual study and worship; prophetic promises, fulfillment of
announcement of shift to, 12–17
authors' experiences with, 159–61
blessings of, 103, 118, 135–45
challenges of, 79–82, 118
during COVID-19 pandemic, 148, 157–59
doctrinal foundations of, 8–12
example of, 93–95
and lasting conversion, 15–16, 30
as prescient, 148
home evening, 75–76, 126
homesickness, 42
hope, in enjoying revelatory experiences, 172–73
horizontal comparison, 60

I

imperfection, of families, 19–20
individual study and worship, 47–48, 64–65. *See also* personal revelatory experiences
balancing stability and creativity in, 59–60
blessings of, 69
careful versus casual, 52
in exemplary family, 62–64
ideas for, 56–59
and implementation of *Come, Follow Me*, 54–55
and lasting conversion, 13–15
members' recent experiences with, 61–62
revelation through, 51–53
inner world, sharing, 4–5, 7
interpersonal revelatory experiences, 3–6
invitation, principle of lived, 63
Israel, gathering of, 179–82
Israelites, 10

J

Jesus Christ, 40, 70, 137–39, 143–45
Jewish Sabbath observance, 75, 100–104
insights on, 105–12
lessons from, 112–13

K

Kelley, Heather Howell, 75, 127
Kelly, Walt, 49
Kimball, Heber C., 31
Kimball, Spencer W., 33

L

Lebow, Jay, 149
Lee, Harold B., 79
lived invitation, principle of, 63
love
for Christ, 143–44
commandment regarding, 136
of God, 186

M

Magic Five Hours, 141
Marks, Larry, 7–8
Marks, Renee, 8
marriage
home-centered learning's impact on, 129–30, 139–42
and Sabbath observance, 111
Mason, Patrick, 51–52
Maxwell, Neal A., 3, 39, 52, 53, 55, 61, 79
McCulloch, James E., 12
McKay, David O., 12
media
and decreased influence of adversary, 129
Sabbath and, 104–5
meetings, 187
Miller, Lisa, 20–21
Monson, Thomas S., 58
mortality, feeling out of place in, 42
Moses, 10, 34, 184
music, 71
Myerhoff, Barbara, 34–35

N

Nelson, Russell M. *See also* prophetic promises, fulfillment of
blessings given by, 145
on commandments, 65
counsel of, for challenging times, 95–96
on covenant path, 182–83

on drawing closer to Lord, 144–45
on gathering of Israel, 179–80, 181
on home-centered gospel learning, xiii, 11–12, 16, 31, 103, 118, 135
on importance of revelation, 30–31
on increasing faith, 30
on optimism for future, 51
on personal spiritual experiences, 31
as prophet, 47
on receiving revelation, 1–2, 50, 96
recurring teachings of, 48
on revelation, 145
on Sabbath, 99
on Satan, 49
on scripture study, 41
on temple work, 185
Nelson, Wendy Watson, 47

O

Oaks, Dallin H., 50, 136, 143
ordinances, 150, 186–87
others
    commandment to love, 136
    seeing, through God's perspective, 39
    serving, 5
ourselves, sharing, 4–5, 7

P

Padilla-Walker, Laura, 104
parents/parenting
    and children's spiritual experiences, 42–43
    equal partnership in, 81
    and family teaching pattern, 8–12, 25–26, 70
    responsibilities of, 95
    revelatory experience regarding, 39–41
    Sabbath observance and relationship with children, 111–12
    as spiritual journey, 20–21
personal revelatory experiences, 1–2, 28–29, 31, 35–37. *See also* individual study and worship
power hour, 58–59
prayer, 51–52, 53
    example of, 62
    family, 72–74, 152–54, 156

pride, in children, 108–10
principle of lived invitation, 63
prodigal children, 176–77
prophetic promises, fulfillment of, 117–18, 135–36
    regarding children's enthusiasm, 122–27
    regarding decrease in Satan's influence, 127–31
    regarding Sabbath, 118–22
prophets and apostles
    blessings of belief in, 187–88
    heeding, 52
    individualized inspiration and revelation for, 47
    insights on revelatory experiences from, 29–33

R

repentance, 51
revelation
    continuation of, 145
    defined, 2–3
    essential issues about receiving, 176
    in family relationships, 174–75
    through individual study and worship, 51–53
    learning about, 148
    learning and increasing capacity to receive, 50, 96
    versus revelatory experiences, 32
    synchronous/asynchronous, 174–75
revelatory experiences. *See also* sacred experiences
    building Zion and, 168–69
    commonalities in, 44
    as constant, 32
    councils and, 170–71
    as encouraged by gathering, 186–87
    faith, hope, and charity in enjoying, 172–74
    in family history and temple work, 169–70
    in family relationships, 165–77
    grandparents and, 167–68
    importance of, 30–31
    insights on, from prophets and apostles, 29–33

revelatory experiences (*continued*)
    insights on, from scriptures, 25–29
    interpersonal, 3–6
    personal, 1–2, 28–29, 31, 35–37
    preparing for, 36
    versus revelation, 32
    shared, 3, 6–7, 26–29, 31–32
    sharing, 6–8, 19
    types of matters addressed in, 171–72
    as yielding eternal life, 175–76
Riess, Jana, 35–36, 51
rigidity, 42–43

S

Sabbath observance, 99–101
    children and ritual of, 75
    as delight, 118–22
    and electronic devices, 104–5
    insights on, 105–12
    Jewish, 101–4
    lessons from Jewish, 112–13
sacrament, during COVID-19 pandemic, 158
sacred experiences. *See also* revelatory experiences
    of Larry Marks, 7–8
    sharing, 4
    writing about, 70
Satan
    promise regarding decreased influence of, 127–31
    reality, power, and cunning of, 48–50
scriptures
    insights on revelatory experiences from, 25–29
    social science support for truths from, 34–37
    studying, 41, 51–52, 53, 62, 176
service, 5
shared revelatory experiences, 3, 6–7, 26–29, 31–32, 33–34, 165–77. *See also* family gospel study
singing, and Sabbath observance, 106
singles, 86–87, 142
Smith, Joseph, 29–30, 64, 100, 186–87
Smith, Joseph F., 34
social science, 16, 34–37
spiritual experiences, 37–44
spiritual fire, 34
spiritual gifts, 165–67
spiritual preparation, 2
synchronous revelation, 174–75

T

technology, 60, 104–5
temples and temple work, 33, 102–3, 169–70, 185, 186–87
time
    for family study, 85
    for individual study and worship, 57
    Sabbath as sanctification of, 102, 110
timing, 174
tithing, 7–8
Top, Brent, 14
trials
    faith while navigating, 38–39, 44
    as growth opportunities, 156–57
    reactions to, 39
    spiritual experiences during, 38–39
truth, receiving, 100

U

Uchtdorf, Dieter F., 19–20

W

ward members, closer connection with, 142–45
washing machine, 7–8
wayward children, 176–77
Widtsoe, John A., 183
women, and gathering of Israel, 181

Y

Young, Brigham, 52

Z

Zion, 168–69, 180
Zoom, 154–55, 156, 160–61

About the Authors

Loren D. Marks joined the Brigham Young University School of Family Life in 2015, after thirteen years at Louisiana State University. Loren received his BS and MS degrees from BYU and his PhD from the University of Delaware. He is a codirector (with David Dollahite) of the American Families of Faith Project and coauthor of *Religion and Families*. Loren and his wife, Sandra, married in 1995 and are the parents of five children.

David C. Dollahite is a professor of family life at Brigham Young University, where he teaches classes and conducts research on the links between religion and family life. He is a codirector (with Loren Marks) of the American Families of Faith Project. He obtained a bachelor's degree in family life and a master's degree in marriage and family therapy from BYU and a doctorate in family studies from the University of Minnesota. David and his wife, Mary, are the parents of seven kids. He is a coauthor of *Strengths in Diverse Families of Faith*.